Nazi Saboteurs on Trial

Nazi Saboteurs on Trial

A Military Tribunal and American Law

LOUIS FISHER

University Press of Kansas

© 2003 by the University Press of Kansas

All rights reserved

Published by the University Press of Kansas (Lawrence, Kansas 66049), which was
organized by the Kansas Board of Regents and is operated and funded by Emporia
State University, Fort Hays State University, Kansas State University, Pittsburg State
University, the University of Kansas, and Wichita State University

Library of Congress Cataloging-in-Publication Data

Fisher, Louis.

  Nazi saboteurs on trial: a military tribunal and American law / Louis
Fisher.

    p. cm.

Includes bibliographical references and index.

  ISBN 0-7006-1238-6 (cloth: alk. paper)

  1. Nazi Saboteurs Trial, Washington, D.C., 1942. 2. Trials
(Sabotage)—Washington, D.C. I. Title.

  KF224.N28 F57 2003

  345.73'0264—dc21   2002152204

British Library Cataloguing in Publication Data is available.

Printed in the United States of America

10 9 8 7 6 5 4 3 2 1

The paper used in this publication meets the minimum requirements of the American
National Standard for Permanence of Paper for Printed Library Materials
Z39.48-1984.

To the Library of Congress,
for more than three decades
my home in so many ways

Contents

Preface

saboteur : 破壊 する (

The landing of eight German saboteurs on the East Coast of the United States in June 1942, placed on shore at night by submarines, electrified the nation. Detailed newspaper coverage followed the quick roundup of the men and President Franklin D. Roosevelt's creation of a military commission to try them. After that, in quick succession, came the dramatic appeal to the U.S. Supreme Court in special summer session; its decision in *Ex parte Quirin,* upholding the jurisdiction of the commission; a finding of guilt for all eight; followed by the execution of six and the sentencing of two to prison. These events, over a period of less than two months, raised important issues. What happens to constitutional values in time of war? Can a President prohibit courts from reviewing his actions as Commander in Chief? May Presidents use military tribunals when civil courts are open and operating?

The military tribunal of 1942, fascinating in itself, bears importantly on controversies of today. On November 13, 2001, President George W. Bush authorized a military tribunal to try non-U.S. citizens who assisted the al Qaeda terrorists and their attacks on the World Trade Center and the Pentagon. Administration officials and their supporters were quick to cite *Ex parte Quirin* as a legitimating precedent for presidential initiatives in time of war. There are always precedents. Was the 1942 experience good enough to repeat and rely on?

The purpose of this book is to explain the mission of the German saboteurs, the judicial process (partly military, partly civilian) used against them, and executive decisions to first exclude the judiciary and then invite the Supreme Court to hear the case. What conflicts occurred within the Administration? How divided were the Justices? Tensions flared again in 1945 when another military tribunal dealt with two saboteurs sent by Germany. This time, because of objections to the 1942 experience, the Administration decided to create an entirely different type of military tribunal. Questions remain. Does *Quirin* lend legitimacy to President Bush's initiative in 2001? What role should Congress play?

This book is a stepping-stone to a more ambitious undertaking: an analysis of military tribunals from George Washington to the present to judge their effectiveness and constitutionality. The second book, to be published next year by the University Press of Kansas, is tentatively entitled *Military Tribunals: The Law of War and Constitutional Rights.* I want to thank Mike Briggs of the University Press of Kansas for supporting both projects. The decision by President Bush in 2001 to revive military tribunals, and a much closer look at *Ex parte Quirin,* quickened my interest and created a wonderful learning experience for me. I hope that much of it will rub off on the reader.

The bibliographical essay and the footnotes underscore my dependence on the collections maintained by the National Archives, the manuscript room of the Library of Congress, the Franklin D. Roosevelt Library at Hyde Park, New York, Clemson University, and the University of Kentucky. As always, the highly talented staff of the Law Library of the Library of Congress managed to locate documents that seemed beyond my reach. I also appreciate the help of a colleague at Congressional Research Service (CRS), Jennifer Elsea. We shared lots of documents and met many times to think through the troubling history and law of military tribunals. As outside readers, it was my good fortune to have the guidance of Michal Belknap and Scott Silliman. Their distinguished careers in the field of military law helped identify many ways of sharpening and deepening sections of the book. My sincere thanks to both. I also appreciate very helpful copyediting by Linda Lotz.

As I move into my thirty-third year with CRS, I express my always conscious appreciation for living in an environment that energizes me with its scholars, vast holdings, and magnificent buildings. Had I at an early age designed the perfect job for me, this would be it: having the time and resources to study issues with care and then to share findings with members of Congress, their staffs, and committees. The Library of Congress and CRS have given me the opportunity to put knowledge in touch with power. A federal appellate judge some years back said that I had been sitting in a "catbird's seat." I plead guilty. For all these reasons I dedicate this book to the Library of Congress.

Note on Citations

Several works and references are abbreviated in the footnotes using the following system:

FDR Library   Franklin D. Roosevelt Library, Hyde Park, New York.

Landmark Briefs   The briefs and oral argument for *Ex parte Quirin* are printed in Volume 39 of *Landmark Briefs and Arguments of the Supreme Court of the United States,* Philip B. Kurland and Gerhard Casper, eds. (Arlington, Va.: University Publications of America, 1975), pp. 295–666.

LC   Manuscript Room, Library of Congress, Washington, D.C.

Military Trial   Transcript of the trial of the Nazi saboteurs held on the fifth floor of the Justice Department from Wednesday, July 8, to Saturday, August 1, 1942. Copies of the 2,967-page transcript are located in several places. I used the one at National Archives, College Park, Maryland, identified as "RG 153, Records of the Office of the Judge Advocate General (Army), Court-Martial Case Files, CM 334178, 1942 German Saboteur Case."

Nazi Saboteurs on Trial

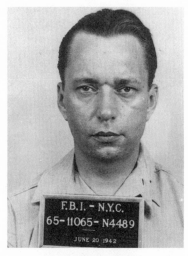

George John Dasch   Ernest Peter Burger

Heinrich Harm Heinck   Richard Quirin

Edward John Kerling

Werner Thiel

Hermann Neubauer

Herbert Haupt

1

School for Saboteurs

detonator : 起爆装置 きばくそうち
fuse : 導火線 どうかせん

Several years before going to war against the United States, Nazi Germany created a training school for saboteurs. By April 1942, the camp was ready to instruct eight Germans in the use of explosives, fuses, and detonators, all to be used against railroads, factories, bridges, and other strategic targets in the United States. Sabotage has a long history. It was being used effectively by all the European powers during World War II. Yet for all the careful planning and preparation, and given Germany's vaunted reputation for precision and efficiency, the operation in the United States fizzled spectacularly. Within a matter of weeks all eight men had been arrested. What went wrong? Was it the training? Poor recruitment? Overwhelming odds? Probably all that and more.

counterespionage: 対 スパイ

"Operation Pastorius"

As an intelligence organization, the *Abwehr* ("defense") dates back to 1866. Over the years it developed skills in counterintelligence and espionage, with functions divided into three branches: Branch I (espionage), Branch II (sabotage and uprisings in foreign countries), and Branch III (counterespionage). Adm. Wilhelm Canaris, a legendary figure in covert operations, was named to head the agency in 1935. Its headquarters in Berlin was located on the Tirpitzufer, a tree-lined street along a canal.[1]

---

1. For background on Canaris, see the opening chapters of Ladislas Farago, The Game of the Foxes: The Untold Story of German Espionage in the United States and

espionage: スパイ *Sabotage: 工場 に 対する 破壊 活動 /行為*
uprising 蜂起

After Adolf Hitler took power in 1933, several Germans in the United States created an organization called the Friends of New Germany. Its purpose was to promote the values and political goals of National Socialism, including racial inequality. For Germans who had become U.S. citizens, their allegiance and loyalty were to be to the Fatherland. The emphasis was on German blood, not on the citizenship one might have acquired. Members were chosen from those of German descent and Aryan blood, "free from Jewish or colored blood."[2] The organization kept the name Friends of New Germany until 1936, when it changed to *Amerika Deutscher Volksbund,* known as the German-American Bund.

Toward the late 1930s, as war loomed, Germany made a concerted effort to have Germans living abroad return home. Part of the incentive was through *Rückwanderer* (returnee, or repatriate) Marks, a form of currency that created a line of credit in Germany. For 1,000 U.S. dollars, one would get something like 4,000 *Rückwanderer* Marks. Individuals entered into this exchange with the understanding that upon returning to Germany they would remain there. Participants in this program would not be eligible for a reentry permit to return to the United States.[3] Some of the eight saboteurs purchased these Marks.

When the position of chief of the Sabotage Division fell vacant in 1939, Canaris turned to Col. Edwin von Lahousen to fill the post.[4] It

Great Britain During World War II (New York: David McKay, 1971); David Kahn, The Final Solution of the Abwehr xi–xv (New York: Garland, 1989); and David Kahn, Hitler's Spies: German Military Intelligence in World War II 226–31 (New York: Macmillan, 1978).

2. U.S. Department of Justice, Criminal Division, "Outline of Evidence: German-American Bund (Amerikadeutscher Volksbund), September 17, 1942, at 66. For other works on the Bund, see Leland V. Bell, In Hitler's Shadow: The Anatomy of American Nazism (Port Washington, N.Y.: Kennikat Press, 1973); Sander A. Diamond, The Nazi Movement in the United States, 1924–1941 (Ithaca, N.Y.: Cornell University Press, 1974); and Susan Canedy, America's Nazis: A Democratic Dilemma, A History of the German American Bund (Menlo Park, Calif.: Markgraf, 1990).

3. Military Trial, at 2484.

4. Charles Wighton & Günter Peis, They Spied on England: Based on the German Secret Service War Diary of General von Lahousen 22–23 (London: Odhams Press, 1958).

was during this period that Germany suffered a painful humiliation called the "Sebold Affair." William G. Sebold, a native of Germany, had traveled to the United States and South America after 1921 to work in industrial and aircraft plants. One of his jobs was with the Consolidated Aircraft Company of San Diego, California. In 1936, he became a naturalized citizen of the United States. During a trip to Germany in 1939 to see his family, the Gestapo asked him to return to the United States as a spy. As added leverage, Gestapo agents said that they knew his real name (Wilhelm George Debowksi, or Debrovksy) and that his maternal grandfather was a Jew. A failure to cooperate, they warned, would result in serious reprisals against Sebold and his family in Germany.[5] A "particularly lurid" message, threatening that he would be "taken care of," described the funeral clothes he would wear "when you're laid out here."[6] Sebold told the American Consulate in Cologne about being pressured to serve as a German agent. His wish, he made clear, was to be loyal to the United States. Soon he was on the road to becoming a double agent.

At the Nazi espionage school in Hamburg, Sebold learned how to microphotograph documents, use secret ink, code and decode, build and operate shortwave radios, and send messages by Morse code. He also received a new name: William (or Harry) Sawyer. With this training he arrived in New York City on February 8, 1940. The FBI set him up in an office at 152 West 42nd Street, where agents installed hidden cameras to photograph visits from German spies. Hidden microphones picked up the conversations. FBI agents listened to plans for the destruction of the General Electric Company in Schenectady, New York.[7] Sebold rented a house in Centerport, Long Island, where FBI agents operated a shortwave radio to send messages to Germany. This operation continued for sixteen months, with the FBI transmitting worthless information and receiving key

5. Art Ronnie, Counterfeit Hero: Fritz Duquesne, Adventurer and Spy 215, 219 (Annapolis, Md.: Naval Institute Press, 1995).

6. "U.S. Bomb Sight Sold to Germany, Spy Jury Is Told," New York Times, September 9, 1941, at 14.

7. "FBI Shows Movies of Spy Rendezvous," New York Times, September 18, 1941, at 13.

details of the German spy ring in the United States.[8] As a result of Sebold's participation and cooperation, thirty-three Nazi spies were arrested, brought to trial on September 3, 1941, and found guilty two months later. Walter Nipkin, another German-born, naturalized U.S. citizen, also helped the FBI as a counterespionage agent.[9]

The convictions marked the end of an important Nazi spy ring headed by Frederick Joubert Duquesne. The loss to Germany from the arrests and prosecutions was profound and stunning. Seeking vital information, it had received nothing of value and had given away much. It had been snookered by its own agents. The essence of the Sebold story was captured by Hollywood in *The House on 92nd Street* (1945), featuring William Eythe as the double agent, Lloyd Nolan as an FBI official, and Leo G. Carroll and Signe Hasso as German spies.

Hitler, furious that more than thirty German spies had been arrested in the United States, confronted Canaris and Lahousen and demanded that they immediately initiate a sabotage plan against America. After this meeting, the two men returned to Berlin, where Canaris told Lahousen: "We'll just have to do it. I know, as you know, that the whole thing is hopeless. But examine every possibility in the light of present circumstances. We have got to make some show of co-operation in this business, and at least demonstrate some good will."[10]

Within a week, Lahousen received a visit from a Lt. Walter Kappe. With much enthusiasm, Kappe reported that he had already identified ten men who had spent years in the United States and were ready to return to America as spies or saboteurs. Canaris and Lahousen felt that the plan was doomed from the start. As Canaris noted, in any undertaking with more than three or four men, "someone always talks."[11] But obviously the project enjoyed strong support from the Gestapo and Party leaders. Canaris and Lahousen shrugged their shoulders and let the program lurch forward.

8. "Spies and Counterspies," New York Times, September 14, 1941, at 2E.
9. "2d FBI 'Spy' Set Snares for Nazi," New York Times, September 27, 1941, at 19.
10. Wighton & Peis, They Spied on England, at 197.
11. Id. at 199.

The goal: Undermine American Productio (handwritten)

With war between Germany and the United States approaching, Kappe had given thought to tapping Germans who lived in the United States or who had once lived there. With easy access to the records of the *Ausland Institut* (Foreign Institute), he studied the backgrounds and experiences of possible candidates. Toward the end of 1941, the Gestapo asked him to establish a sabotage school that would prepare men to conduct covert operations in the United States. The goal: undermine American productivity. To move the project along, he opened an office at 8 Rankestrasse in Berlin and pretended to publish *Der Kaukasus* (Caucasus), a periodical designed to reach German troops fighting in Russia. A copper sign at the entrance read *Schriftleitung "Der Kaukasus"* (Editorial Office of the *Kaukasus*).[12] In fact, the periodical did not exist. It served as a front for his sabotage school. Candidates for the training met with Kappe at the Rankestrasse office for a final screening.

Kappe, familiar with the catastrophe of the Sebold affair, knew all too well the risks of sending spies and saboteurs to the United States. This time, with proper recruitment and training, he hoped to develop a successful program and avoid the mistakes of the past. The training took place at a sabotage school located on the Quenz farm near Brandenburg, about thirty-five miles west of Berlin. Kappe had a long history with the Freikorps in 1922, the Nazi Party, and German-American Bund activities in the United States. After arriving in the United States in 1925, he acquired some skills and experience in newspaper reporting and eventually became editor of the Bund newspaper, *Deutcher Weckruf und Beobachte*r (German Wake-up and Observer). As a frequent lecturer in German-American circles, he met several of the men who would later join his school for saboteurs. In 1937, Kappe returned to Germany to become propaganda director of Station DJB in Berlin.

The sabotage plan for the United States became known as "Operation Pastorius," named after Franz Daniel Pastorius, an early German immigrant to America. He had been the leader of thirteen Quaker families who arrived in Philadelphia in 1683 and had

12. Military Trial, at 2567.

helped develop a German settlement called Germantown in Pennsylvania.[13] Pastorius and his followers fought against slavery and
helped outlaw it in German religious communities. How ironic that
Kappe should select the name Pastorius to help promote the Nazi
ideology of a master race.

The Eight Finalists

Of the eight Germans eventually chosen to go to America for sabotage, Kappe worked first with George John Dasch and had him in
mind as one of two group leaders. Dasch had lived in America from
1922 to 1941 and spoke English fairly well. In March 1941, he left
the United States and returned to Germany, where he monitored
American broadcasts and translated them. In this line of work he
met Kappe on June 3, 1941, and, at Kappe's request, drafted a five-
page plan for espionage and sabotage. Dasch's memo described
three kinds of sabotage—political, industrial, military—and included at least two pages on military sabotage.[14]

Dasch suggested one name as a possible saboteur: Werner Thiel.
Dasch had met him on a boat from the United States to Japan, on
their way back to Germany. About this time, Dasch learned of Edward John Kerling, who would become the other group leader. By
March 1, 1942, Dasch was studying the personal histories of other
possible candidates. Most of them had lived ten to fourteen years in
the United States and were members of either the Bund or the Nazi
Party. From this raw material would be selected about twelve individuals, with the understanding that several would either voluntarily drop out or be asked to leave because they were unsuitable.

Dasch ended up with three members on his team: Ernest Peter
Burger, Heinrich Harm Heinck, and Richard Quirin. He had no previous relationship with any of them. Burger was the only one of

13. Albert Bernhardt Faust, Francis Daniel Pastorius and the 250th Anniversary of
the Founding of Germantown (Philadelphia: Carl Schurz Memorial Foundation,
1934).

14. Military Trial, at 1078.

Dasch's group with military experience. Unlike Dasch, all were members of the Nazi Party. Kerling's group included Hermann Neubauer, Werner Thiel, and Herbert Haupt. The youngest member of the eight, Haupt, was only twenty-two. He was the only one of Kerling's group who was not a member of the Nazi Party. The three weeks at the sabotage camp did little to knit them into a cohesive group. Confidence in one another never developed, and certainly not toward Dasch.

George John Dasch. Born in Speyer on the Rhine, Germany, on February 7, 1903, Dasch entered a Catholic convent at age thirteen to study for the priesthood.[15] About a year later, during World War I, he volunteered with the German Army and was sent to northern France. After the war he returned to the convent, but by 1921 he was eager to leave the country. He failed to board an outgoing steamer from Rotterdam because he had neither papers nor experience as a seaman. Unable to find work, he went to Hamburg and was once again prevented from boarding a steamer. After some jobs as a painter and work in the coal mines, he managed to board the S.S. *Schoharie,* bound for America, and hid in a storeroom. In the status of stowaway he arrived in Philadelphia in October 1922.

Most of his employment after that was in New York City working for a caterer, in the kitchen of restaurants, and as a fry cook. By saving money he was able to return to Europe and come back legally as a candidate for U.S. citizenship. After enlisting in the U.S. Army in 1927, he was sent to Honolulu, where he served in the Aviation Corps. After one year, one month, and ten days, he was discharged. Other jobs ranged from soda fountain clerk to waiter. In 1930, he married Rose Marie Guille. They often worked at the same hotel, she as a beautician and he as a waiter. In 1932, Dasch relocated to Chicago as a salesman of sanctuary supplies for Catholic churches and institutions, but he soon returned to the New York City area and continued to work as a waiter. As he notes in his book, "Even if I

15. At the military tribunal, Dasch described in great detail his early years in Germany. Id. at 1027–32.

wanted to I couldn't hide the fact that I never amounted to very much."[16] This sense of inadequacy helps explain his conduct when he reached America with the other saboteurs.

According to Dasch's testimony before the military tribunal, he had opposed Nazism, Hitler, and the German-American Bund. He said that his mother's visit in June 1939, bringing positive news about conditions in Germany, and the German-Russian nonaggression pact in August 1939 caused him to rethink his position.[17] This part of the story is confusing. In his book he claims that the United States "was my country. I was proud of it. I never thought of myself as a German any more."[18] Still, he chose to return to Germany. Having filed his final U.S. citizenship papers, paid the fees, and passed the examinations, he nevertheless decided when war broke out on September 3 to make the arduous journey back to Germany. By March 1941, he was on the Japanese steamer *Tatuta Maru,* bound for Honolulu and Japan. About forty Germans were on the boat. One was Werner Thiel.

From Japan, Dasch proceeded across the Manchurian mainland to Russia and on to Berlin, arriving there May 13. He registered with the foreign association, the *Ausland Institut.* Shortly after that, he was in touch with Lieutenant Kappe. Dasch testified that he had not known Kappe in the United States. However, one of Dasch's connections was Reinhold Barth, husband of his first cousin. Barth, in close contact with Kappe, served as an instructor at the sabotage school.

Ernest Peter Burger. In many ways, Dasch seems poles apart from Burger. While Dasch irritated almost everyone at the tribunal with his verbosity, irrelevant meanderings, and condescending airs, Burger drew uniform praise for being direct, factual, and accurate. Yet Dasch and Burger had formed a close friendship by the time they reached their hotel in New York City, using the time to share

16. George J. Dasch, Eight Spies Against America 17 (New York: Robert M. McBride, 1959).
17. Military Trial, at 1042–45.
18. Dasch, Eight Spies Against America, at 18.

misgivings about the sabotage operation and conditions in Nazi Germany. After a long and heartfelt discussion, they agreed to turn themselves in and betray the others. Dasch provided the leadership, but Burger never wavered in his support.

Born on September 1, 1906, in Augsburg, Bavaria, Burger attended a machine vocational institute after high school and worked throughout Germany as a machine builder. He joined the Nazi Party and participated in the "Beer Hall Putsch" of 1923, which sent Hitler to prison and gave him the time to write *Mein Kampf.*[19] This early relationship with Hitler did not help Burger, because he ended up in the wrong wing of the Party: the brown-shirted SA (*Sturm Abteiling,* or Storm Troopers). Hitler later decided that he needed a personal bodyguard: the black-uniformed SS (*Schutzstaffel,* or protection guard). Starting out with a few hundred men, the SS grew in political strength under Heinrich Himmler, who later consolidated his power by heading the secret police, the Gestapo.

In February 1927, Burger left Germany for the United States. He worked in Wisconsin as a tool maker and later in Illinois with a motor repair department. In Illinois, he declared his intention to become a U.S. citizen. He went back to Germany in 1929 for a four-week visit, and upon his return to the United States, he found employment as a tool and die maker in Detroit, where he enlisted in the Michigan National Guard. Honorably discharged because he was moving to Milwaukee, he joined the Wisconsin National Guard. In 1933, after becoming a U.S. citizen, he decided to return to Germany. He first went to Munich and worked with the Chief Adjutant's Office, attached to Chief of Staff Ernst Röhm. At that time, Röhm was extremely close to Hitler, but on June 30, 1934, fortunes changed. With Hitler's backing, Röhm and hundreds of Storm Troopers were shot and killed by the SS. Burger survived the purge because he had been assigned to the Chief of the Medical Corps, but his SA background would cause him problems with the Gestapo.

At the University of Berlin, Burger took courses in journalism and geopolitics and received his diploma in July 1939. One week after

19. Military Trial, at 2596–97.

graduation he married Bettina Luscher, his secretary. On March 4, 1940, he was arrested by the Gestapo and held for seventeen months: five months at a prison in Poland, five to six weeks in a cellar of the Gestapo headquarters in Berlin, and a year in the building of the Central Police Headquarters in Berlin. The government charged him with falsification of papers. Although those charges were eventually dropped after four times in court, the Gestapo visited his pregnant wife and told her that Burger had stolen money in Vienna and would spend eight years with a chain gang. She knew it was a lie, because Burger had never been in Vienna, but under this constant pressure and strain, she suffered a breakdown and a miscarriage.[20]

Burger, finally released on July 22, 1941, did guard duty over Yugoslavian and English prisoners. He was advised that, because of the Gestapo reports, he would have no chance of promotion in the Army. He testified before the military tribunal that he had volunteered to attend the sabotage school to "rehabilitate" himself. About April 5, 1942, he turned in his uniform and reported in civilian clothes to the Quenz farm.

Heinrich Harm Heinck. At the military tribunal, defense counsel Col. Kenneth Royall described Heinck as "a fellow who follows orders" and stated that there was no possibility of him ever "originating anything" or taking any action on his own initiative.[21] Born in Hamburg on June 27, 1907, Heinck worked in the machine shop at the Hamburg-American Shipping Company and also on the S.S. *Westphalia* as an oiler and machinist's helper. On a trip to New York in 1926, he jumped ship and entered the country without legal papers. Most of his jobs in America were as a tool and die maker, but he also worked in restaurants and hotels and as a chauffeur. In 1933, he married Anna Isabella Goetz, who lived in New York City.

In 1934, Heinck joined the German-American Bund in New York City and heard Walter Kappe give speeches four or five times. Heinck's last job was with the American Machine Tool Company, a

20. Id. at 344–45, 2600–2.
21. Id. at 2817.

branch of a firm that made the Norden bombsight. In 1939, there was talk of all noncitizens having to leave the factory because of contracts the company had with the federal government. Heinck returned to Germany at that point and worked at the Volkswagenwerk factory in Braunschweig as a tool maker. He met Richard Quirin at the factory and also joined the Nazi Party. His wife accompanied him to Germany and lived in the south with her parents and young son.

In October 1941, Heinck went to the Ausland Organization (AO) to check into the possibility of returning to the United States. Kappe came to the AO and addressed a meeting of men like Heinck and Quirin who had spent time in America. Someone at the factory asked Heinck whether he would be interested in going to the United States as part of a team to stop or slow down production at American factories. Quirin came to Heinck's house, and they talked about the proposal. Shortly after that, they received a typewritten letter from Kappe, telling them to go to the farm near Brandenburg.

Richard Quirin. Born in Berlin on April 26, 1908, Quirin did not know his father's name, so he took his mother's maiden name. She left him with foster parents when he was two. At age twelve he went to Hanover to live with his mother, and two years later he left school to become a mechanic's helper. Later he worked on a farm. He came to America in 1927 to see his uncle in Schenectady, attended night school to learn English, and worked for General Electric for three years before being laid off. At that point he moved to New York City and worked at various jobs.

In 1936, he married Anna Sesselmann, who had been born in Germany. The two worked for J. W. Rauch in Chappaqua, New York in early 1938, he as chauffeur and she as housekeeper. In 1933, he joined the Friends of New Germany and also the Nazi Party. In 1939, after buying some *Rückwanderer* Marks, he returned to Germany with his wife and began working with Volkswagenwerk in Braunschweig.[22] His daughter, Rosemarie, was born

22. Id. at 2463–65.

October 4, 1940. He and Heinck left Braunschweig and traveled together to the farm near Brandenburg.

Edward John Kerling. As the second group leader, Kerling returned to the United States in 1942 as part of the saboteur team to
confront what his defense counsel called a "triangular matrimonial
difficulty" involving his wife and girlfriend.[23] Born in Wiesbaden
on June 12, 1909, Kerling joined the Nazi Party in 1928. His low
membership number of 70,000—being under 100,000—gave him
"special status in the Party." He left Germany in March 1928 to
come to the United States, settling in New York City. After several
years of work smoking hams at a packing house in Brooklyn, and
later with a packing house in Manhattan as a shipping clerk, he
served as chauffeur for Eli Culbertson, a bridge expert, in Hicks-
ville, Long Island.

On October 31, 1931, he married Marie Sichart, who had come
to the United States from Munich in the 1920s. They went to Germany in 1933 for a couple of months but returned to New York
City. He then worked as chauffeur for W. J. Hoggson, a banker, who
lived in Greenwich, Connecticut. Later he worked for Victor C.
Armstrong, a railroad executive. While working in Florida he met
his girlfriend, Hedwig Engemann. Marie asked for a divorce so that
he could marry Hedy and have children. Behind Marie's generous
offer was likely her reluctance to leave the United States and go to
Germany, as her husband hoped to do. By the late 1930s, she
seemed to regard Kerling more as a brother than a husband.[24]

When war broke out in Europe in September 1939, Kerling and
several of his friends bought a yacht, the *Lekala,* with the plan of
sailing it to Germany. Another theory was that they planned to use
the boat to carry supplies to German raiders off the Atlantic Coast.
After running into problems with the Coast Guard and the FBI, they
sold the boat in Miami. In June 1940, Kerling returned to Germany
by taking a boat to Lisbon, flying to Rome, and going by train to

23. Id. at 2816.
24. Id. at 2310, 2721–22, 2735.

Innsbruck, arriving on August 3, 1940. His wife remained in New York City. After reaching Berlin, Kerling joined an army listening post in Deauville, France, and translated English broadcasts. After about three months he landed a job with the Propaganda Ministry, responsible for managing German theaters and stage shows. He remained there until April 1942, when Kappe persuaded him to join the others at the sabotage school.

Hermann Neubauer. The only one wounded in action as a soldier was Neubauer. Born in Hamburg on February 5, 1910, he attended public schools and apprenticed as a cook. He came to the United States in 1931 and worked as a cook in various hotels and on ships. His work with shipping lines took him to England, Australia, and South America. Neubauer joined the German-American Bund in 1935 or early 1936 but had to resign because the Bund was restricted to U.S. citizens. In 1936, he purchased $1,000 (4,000 Marks) of *Rückswanderer,* which gave him a line of credit in Germany and committed him to staying there.

In 1937, Neubauer joined the Nazi Party. He also applied for U.S. citizenship and sent in his papers, but he learned that his eligibility had expired just one day before his application for citizenship. On January 10, 1940, he married Alma Wolf, who had been born in the United States. Later that year, Neubauer met Kerling, Heinck, and several other people and decided to return to Germany by buying the *Lekala* and sailing it home. When that plan fell through, Neubauer boarded the S.S. *Exochorda* with Kerling and traveled to Germany via Lisbon and Rome, arriving on August 3, 1940.

After seeing his parents, he was drafted into the German Army in November and sent to fight on the Eastern Front. During bombardment by the Russians in the summer of 1941, he received shell splinters over his right eye and in his right cheek and left leg. He remained in a hospital in Stuttgart until November 1941, carrying scars and embedded splinters. For two days he lost the ability to speak, and even after his recovery he was still excitable and nervous about any noise. Over a six-month period he was in and out of hospitals and medical centers.[25] While he was convalescing, officials asked him about his knowledge of the United States and facility with English. At a hospital in Vienna, he received a letter from Kappe asking if he would go to the United States on a special assignment. After joining his wife and family at Hamburg, he traveled to the school outside Brandenburg.

Werner Thiel. At the military tribunal, Thiel's defense counsel described him as a fairly passive individual who took orders: "If possible, he is even more incapable than Heinck was for carrying anything out on his own initiative."[26] Thiel was born in Essen on March 29, 1907. After school he apprenticed as a machinist in repair shops at railroad yards and worked at a small firm making bicycle equipment. Later, unable to find work, he was supported by his parents until coming to the United States in 1927. He worked as a tool and die maker with Ford Motor Company in Michigan and later for Detroit Bodies. He plugged along with short-term and seasonal work, followed by layoffs, and moved from Michigan to Indiana, California, Pennsylvania, and Florida. In New York City, he worked as a porter and handyman at a home for the old and infirm. He joined the Friends of New Germany in 1933, became active with the German-American Bund, and joined the Nazi Party in 1939. In March 1941, he sailed to Toyko on the *Tatuta Maru,* eventually traveling on to Russia and arriving in Berlin in May 1941. One his fellow passengers on the *Tatuta Maru* was Dasch. Thiel said that he had known Burger in the United States while working as a tool and die maker in Detroit.

Upon his return to Germany, Thiel worked with a small company as a screw machine setup man from July 1941 to April 1, 1942. One night he attended a meeting of the Ausland group, where he met Dasch and Kappe. He had heard Kappe speak in Chicago in 1934 at a meeting of the Friends of New Germany. A few days later, Dasch met with Thiel at a small bar in West Berlin and asked him to

25. Id. at 1724–25, 2198–99.
26. Id. at 2820.

join a group of people who would help the Fatherland by returning to the United States. When Thiel agreed to go to the sabotage school, he was still recovering from the shock of having one brother killed in action and another who lost his left eye in combat.

Herbert Haupt. By far the youngest member of the group, Haupt was born in Germany on December 21, 1919, in Stettin. His father came to the United States in 1923, and two years later, Herbert came with his mother. Since both parents became naturalized U.S. citizens, he was an American citizen. After school, he got a job as an apprentice for Simpson's Optical Company in Chicago, with the goal of becoming an optical worker. He began dating Gerda Stuckmann Melind, whose husband had died after five months of marriage. In June 1941, she told Haupt that she was pregnant and that he was the father. Despite promising not to desert her, he was soon on his way to Mexico with two friends.

Unable to find work in Mexico or to obtain a passport for Nicaragua for possible work there, Haupt agreed to accept passage from the German Consul in Mexico City to go to Japan for a job at a monastery. There is some evidence that German agents in Mexico City approached Haupt and asked him to return to Germany to participate in a sabotage operation. Upon reaching Japan, Haupt discovered that the monastery was more of a labor camp with poor conditions and sanitation. He went to Kobi for training as a sailor, eventually leaving on a ship bound for Germany. After sailing around Cape Horn and surviving a British blockade (receiving two medals for his work as oiler and lookout in the crow's nest), he arrived in Bordeaux, France, on the same day that Germany declared war on the United States. He testified that he had been questioned repeatedly by Gestapo agents, who thought that he might be a U.S. spy. Released, he went to Saarbrucken and from there stayed with his grandmother, Anna Froehling, in Stettin.

Haupt received a letter from Kappe inviting him to come to Berlin to tell the story of his adventurous trip from Mexico to Germany. At Rankestrasse, he met Kappe, told his story, and returned home to Stettin. Kappe later contacted him about taking a trip to the United

States and reminded Haupt that his mother's brother, Otto Froehling, was in a concentration camp. The gentle hint was that if Haupt
went to the United States and told his uncle, Walter Froehling, about
Walter's brother Otto, Haupt could be assured of Walter's cooperation. Haupt returned to Berlin and met Dasch.

Several other trainees at the Quenz farm did not make the trip to
America. One was Ernst Zuber, who had come to the school from
the Russian front after having a nervous breakdown. Within a short
time he announced that he lacked the mental or physical skills to
take part in the operation and left. Another candidate was Joseph
Schmidt, known as "Smitty" or by his pseudonym, Jerry Swenson.
Haupt had met Schmidt in Mexico City and knew that he had spent
time in Canada. Schmidt completed the training and was supposed
to leave with Group 1, under Dasch. However, when they were
about to board the submarine, Schmidt told Kappe that he had a ve-
nereal disease and would have to go to a hospital for treatment. It is
uncertain whether Schmidt was really infected. He may have been
looking for an excuse to exit from the venture, perhaps because he
thought that he was more qualified than Dasch to lead a group.
There was also a third person by the name of "Scotty" who did not
last long.

Instruction and Training

The Quenz farm, located near Brandenburg, was well equipped to
serve as a sabotage school. It had a main house, where the men slept
and ate, and several outlying buildings, including a two-story gym-
nasium, a garage, a greenhouse (to grow vegetables, fruit, and flow-
ers), and two outdoor shooting ranges (one for pistol and the other
for rifle). On the top floor of the garage, one room was used for class-
work and another for the laboratory. A person named "Bill Dempsey" taught them gymnastics. He had been a prizefighter in the
United States and borrowed the name of the great Jack Dempsey.

During their three weeks at the school, the saboteurs-to-be followed a regular schedule. They awoke at 7 a.m., did calisthenics

until 7:30, made up their bunks, and had breakfast at 8:00. They were expected to practice their English by reading American newspapers and magazines and conversing in English. During classes in the morning (9:00 to 12:00) and afternoon (2:00 to 4:00), they learned about explosives, fuses, and timing devices. Those lectures were given in German by two professors, Dr. Walter Schultze and Dr. Helmuth Koenig. Classes ranged from general chemistry to distinctions between light-burning mixtures (lit by a match) and hard-burning mixtures (requiring a fuse). Reinhold Barth gave lectures on American railroad systems and identified the main terminal points and vulnerable targets, such as bottlenecks. He pointed out weak spots on boxcars and switching devices.

After the afternoon classes, the men participated in soccer, boxing, wrestling, and other sports. After dinner at six, they discussed what they had learned that day. Whatever notes they took were confiscated, because all instruction had to be memorized. Saturday mornings were devoted to a general review of the work. Saturday afternoons and Sundays were free, and some of the men went for bicycle rides or took trips into Berlin. On some weekday evenings, Kappe accompanied the men to a local tavern for drinks and dinner. As they walked along the road, the students would break into their American repertoire of songs, including "The Star-Spangled Banner" and "Oh, Susanna!"[27] The neighbors must have wondered. The hours at the tavern gave Kappe an opportunity to see how well the men handled their liquor. Most drank in moderation, but Heinck's conduct indicated that he might not know when to say "enough."

On one of those evenings, Dasch and Burger walked a couple hundred yards ahead of the others. Dasch, who had read about Burger's seventeen months in prison under the Gestapo, asked for his version of what had happened. Burger began emotionally, "That dirty Nazi Himmler . . . ," at which point Dasch stopped him: "That is enough. Please keep quiet. Don't say nothing no more. The day and the time will come when I will reopen it again to you; but now

27. Eugene Rachlis, They Came to Kill 47 (New York: Random House, 1961).

do me a favor and say nothing, not even that I asked you. Forget it."[28] When the two settled into their hotel rooms in New York City, the conversation would continue.

Practical exercises required the students to use explosives on wooden posts buried in sand and iron tracks laid on the ground. They learned that two pounds of explosives would cut a railroad rail. The explosives they took to the United States included lumps of TNT that looked like pieces of coal; these could be put in the furnaces of railroad locomotives or coal-burning furnaces to crack and ruin the boilers. They learned about the destructive effect of placing sand or emery dust in the bearings and machinery of trains and factories. Another part of the instruction included the dynamiting of department stores operated by Jews.

As part of the training, Kerling and Haupt were put in a kayak to practice the transfer from submarine to shore. The kayak capsized in the icy water, and both men, weighted down with clothing and boots, struggled to survive. That experience convinced Kappe to abandon kayaks in favor of rubber boats manned by the submarine crew.

The men studied U.S. maps to learn the locations of aluminum and magnesium plants, bridges, tunnels, and waterways. The two groups were assigned different tasks. Dasch's group would concentrate on aluminum plants at Alcoa, Tennessee; East St. Louis; Massina, New York; and the cryolite plant of the Aluminum Company at Philadelphia. They would also sabotage the locks of the Ohio River between Pittsburgh and Louisville. Kerling and his men would devote their efforts to railroads: the Pennsylvania Railroad station at Newark, the Hell Gate Bridge in New York, and the Chesapeake & Ohio Railroad. On April 29 and 30, the students were given a practical test to destroy designated targets on the farm. The instructors did what they could to unnerve the students, including tossing firecrackers at them.

All eight men were asked to create false names for themselves. Dasch suggested that they keep their first names but create last

28. Military Trial, at 2530.

names by using the first two letters of their real names.[29] He picked
the name "George John Davis." Below are their names and ages at
the time they landed in America. Burger insisted on keeping his
own name because he carried documents with that name. Although
Haupt chose a pseudonym (the name of his best friend in the United
States), he never used it. Other than Dasch and Haupt, all were
members of the Nazi Party.

GROUP 1

George John Dasch (39)	"George John Davis"
Ernest Peter Burger (35)	Ernest Peter Burger
Heinrich Harm Heinck (34)	"Henry Kaynor"
Richard Quirin (34)	"Richard Quintas"

GROUP 2

Edward John Kerling (33)	"Edward J. Kelly"
Herbert Haupt (22)	"Lawrence Jordan"
Hermann Neubauer (32)	"Henry Nicholas"
Werner Thiel (35)	"William Thomas"

Some of the men picked up code names as agents of German Intelligence. From the verb *vertrauen* (to put one's trust in someone),
they were familiar with the noun *Vertrauensmann,* or *V-Mann,* a
term used widely for someone trusted as an intermediary. In the
context of the saboteur school, and as written into the contracts they
signed, the term meant an agent for the Intelligence Service. Dasch
received the V-name "Stritch," which might have been a pun, because *Stritch* in German means a line or dash. Haupt's V-name was
"Bingo."

After creating false names, the men were asked to manufacture
elaborate if juvenile tales about themselves. Neubauer would say
that he was an American born in Walsten, Pennsylvania. His

29. Id. at 1091.

mother, so the story went, had returned to Lithuania, where she and his father were from. The choice of Walsten came from Dasch, whose wife had been born there. Thiel was supposedly born in Chicago but raised in Switzerland. Dasch thought that Burger's nose made him look Jewish and that his last name would pass for Jewish, so Burger would accompany the others as a Jewish refugee. Dasch's new birthplace became San Francisco, before the earthquake and fire; he had therefore "lost" all his personal documents. Someone decided that Quirin looked Hispanic, so he became "Quintas," born in Lisbon but leaving with his parents at an early age to go to the United States. Armed with these far-fetched stories, the men were urged to talk about their new identities until they felt at home with them.

Classes and practical work ended on April 30, followed by vacation from May 1 to May 12, when the students visited their families and wives to say good-bye, without, of course, saying anything about their training or destination. The men reported back to the school to receive instructions in writing with secret ink, both on cloth and on paper. One technique immersed a piece of paper in a dish of water until it was thoroughly soaked. The paper was then lifted by two of the corners to prevent wrinkling and placed on a flat glass surface, with a dry sheet over it, on which one wrote with a black pencil with sufficient pressure to touch the sheet underneath. The wet sheet was left on the glass until thoroughly dry. The invisible writing would appear once the paper was placed back in water.

To write on cloth, one used a teaspoon of alcohol mixed in a glass with a dissolved laxative pill (such as Ex-Lax). The invisible writing became red when exposed to fumes from ammonia (ammonium hydroxide). This technique was used on two handkerchiefs and given to Dasch and Kerling as group leaders. The handkerchiefs contained the names and addresses of people in the United States and also a contact point in Lisbon, Portugal, allowing the two leaders to reach Kappe. Prosecutors at the military tribunal used this information to show that the saboteurs—at least the two group leaders—had been sent to spy on the United States and send military secrets back to Germany.

Kappe had another technique for staying in touch with the saboteurs. As a front, Burger was to become a commercial artist and place ads in the *Chicago Tribune* on the first and fifteenth of each month, giving his name, address, and availability for work. Since he could play the violin, he would also use the ad to promote himself as a violin teacher.[30] Kappe could read these ads to learn that the group was functioning and in touch with one another.

Upon their return to Berlin, the students spent three days visiting aluminum plants, railroad yards, and canal locks. At the plants of I. G. Farben, they learned that aluminum plants work on electrical power and can be disabled by striking the high-tension poles carrying power to the plants. By interrupting power for eight hours, the contents of the stove and bath would congeal, rendering them useless. After inspecting canal systems to understand the vulnerable points of inland waterways, they toured railroad yards to find similar weaknesses: bearings, switches, brakes, and engines.

On May 20, the students and their instructors met at a private room in the Restaurant Tiergarten in Berlin for a farewell banquet. The group was in high spirits, buoyed by encouraging remarks from Kappe and the two group leaders. Yet the undercurrents were not good. There was little confidence among the eight toward one another. They worried about Dasch's competence and commitment, Burger's terrible experience with the Gestapo, Neubauer's emotional and physical stability, Heinck's drinking problem, and Haupt's appetite for money, which might cause him to double-cross the group.

To Paris and Lorient

May 21 was a free day in Berlin. At noon the next day, Kappe and his team of saboteurs boarded an express train for Paris, arriving there at eight in the morning and registering at the Deux Monde Hotel on the Avenue de L'Opera. For several days it was fun and

30. Id. at 412.

games, including as much sightseeing at they could manage. Heinck, having had too much to drink, told people at the hotel bar that he was a secret agent. Haupt caused a ruckus one evening when he refused to pay a prostitute. When she began screaming in French, alarming the neighbors, his colleagues raced to the scene and paid her for her services.

At the military tribunal, Burger testified that Dasch had met with someone in Paris (Dasch claimed that it was an American journalist) to disclose his plans to turn himself in to the FBI when he reached America. Dasch made the same claim to the tribunal. Whether this story is true is impossible to say. There might be something to it, or Dasch and Burger could have concocted the story while sitting in their hotel room in New York City, knowing that the account would bolster Dasch's claim that he had come to America to do no harm.

By the evening of May 25, the men were on a train for Lorient, on the French coast, to board the submarines. They arrived about noon the next day and checked in at the Hotel Jour de Rêve. On this leg of the journey, Dasch lost a pocketbook that contained his Social Security card and photos of his mother, wife, and himself. He also left a pipe behind. Dasch reported the loss to the police, but when he was unable to produce identification papers for himself, the police alerted the Gestapo. Dasch, hoping to keep the matter quiet, had to call Kappe to explain what had happened. Kappe, arriving to settle the dispute, was furious with Dasch. He wondered again about Dasch's competence and seriousness.

Other problems emerged. When Kappe distributed American money to the eight men, they noticed that the $50 bills were in series. U.S. authorities would know that the bills came from the same group and would be instantly suspicious. Kappe acknowledged the blunder and told them not to cash more than one bill at a time. As the men looked through the money, they saw that some of it was in gold certificates. America had gone off the gold standard in 1933, making the certificates not only useless but illegal—a sure giveaway that the bearers were up to no good. The men were so upset by Kappe's carelessness that some wanted to bail out of the operation.

The trial before the tribunal disclosed that Kappe and Dasch argued about two issues. First, Kappe wanted the two groups to begin sabotage operations immediately "in a small way." Dasch insisted that they wait for several months before attempting any sabotage. He prevailed on that point and used it as evidence that he had deliberately postponed operations to give him time to turn the group in. Second, Kappe assigned Burger to be Heinck's partner. Dasch, wanting Burger to go with him, prevailed on that issue as well.

With these problems patched up, or seemingly so, the eight men prepared to go from the hotel to the harbor. Kappe thought that they would arouse less suspicion if they boarded the submarines in uniform than if they wore civilian clothes. Kerling's group left first, on May 26, and Dasch's group left two days later. Kappe told them to wear German uniforms when they landed on the shores of America, because if they were caught immediately, they would be treated as prisoners of war (POWs) rather than spies. They understood that captured spies faced a mandatory death sentence. Members of the group who were not German soldiers (everyone other than Burger and Neubauer) were supposedly assigned to various units of the German Army to bolster the POW pretext. If they reached the beach safely and undetected, they were to change into civilian clothes and put their uniforms in a sack and return it to the submarine.

2

Misadventures in America

Training at the camp carried an air of unreality. Planning to commit sabotage is not the same as doing it. The need to confront reality was delayed by the vacation in early May and the pleasant days in Paris. Now, sitting in the cramped quarters of the submarine, suffering from nausea for the first few days, reality began to hit home. According to their testimony at the military tribunal, several of the saboteurs began to have second thoughts during the long passage to America. Upon their arrival they would have third thoughts.

Surprise at Amagansett

The submarine carrying Dasch and his team took about two weeks to make the trip across the Atlantic. As they approached America, Dasch gave each member of the team a money belt containing about $4,000 in cash. Each man also received $419 in small change to be used for initial purchases. Burger noticed that Quirin and Heinck seemed to be making some plans of their own because they would stop talking whenever he or Dasch walked by. Evidently the "team" was fraying at the edges. Soon it would be every man for himself.

By 8 p.m. on Friday, June 12, they were only twenty miles off Long Island. The sub approached the shore until it bumped against the sand. By coming to the surface, it was able to move forward for some distance, but again it touched sand. The captain swung the submarine around parallel to the shore, in case he needed to depart quickly if attacked. Shortly after midnight, Dasch and his men came up on deck and got into the rubber boat, weighted down with the four boxes of explosives. Two members of the crew paddled them to shore. An attached rope would guide them back to the sub. As the boat neared the beach, waves nearly capsized them, but they made it safely to shore. They planned to change into civilian clothes, place the military outfits in a duffel bag, and return it to the sub with the two crew members.

On the submarine, Dasch had received instructions that if they encountered a patrol on the beach they should overpower it, with the help of the two sailors, and take the patrollers to the submarine. The captives would then be released at some other spot along the coast. Dasch and his men also understood that they were to check their pockets (both uniforms and civilian clothes) for anything of German origin and leave those items on the submarine. Of these two instructions, Dasch decided not to comply with the first, and Burger disobeyed the second.

As Dasch's group began unloading the raft and changing clothes, Dasch noticed in the heavy fog someone walking toward them. It was John C. Cullen, a Coast Guardsman. Instead of directing his men and the two sailors to overpower Cullen, Dasch approached him and asked, "Coast Guard?" Cullen answered, "Yes, sir," and asked Dasch who he was. Dasch told him that they were fishermen from Southampton and had gotten lost. They planned to stay on the beach until sunrise, "and then we will be all right." Cullen told Dasch that he and his men should follow him back to the station house. Dasch refused, saying that he and his friends lacked permits to fish. Cullen insisted that they come along. During this conversation, Burger approached within a few feet and said something in German, provoking Dasch to lash out, "You damn fool, why don't you go back to the other guys?"[1]

Turning to Cullen, Dasch tried a soft sell. He asked Cullen how old he was and whether he had a father and mother at home. When

---

1. Military Trial, at 100–5, 1115–16.

Cullen said that he did, Dasch asked, "You would like to see them, wouldn't you?" adding, "Well, I wouldn't want to kill you." Telling Cullen to forget what he had seen, Dasch offered him about $100 as encouragement. When Cullen said that he did not want the money, Dasch increased the amount to about $300. Later, when counted at the Coast Guard station, the wad of money turned out to be $260.

While Cullen thought about what to do, Dasch said that Cullen would be hearing about him from Washington. Giving his name as George John Davis, he asked for Cullen's name, who replied, "Frank Collins, sir." Cullen decided to take the money and head back to the station, but Dasch stopped him. Taking off his hat, Dasch said, "Take a good look at me. Look in my eyes." Afraid to be hypnotized, Cullen told reporters that he "stared just above his eyes and didn't look into them." Dasch asked Cullen whether he would recognize him if he saw him again. Cullen said that he would not.[2]

In the middle of this conversation, Cullen noticed someone dragging a bag through the sand. It was Burger, deliberately leaving a mark on the beach to lead U.S. authorities to the boxes. Burger also took out of his pockets items with German writing, including a bottle of schnapps and a package of German cigarettes, and placed them in conspicuous places on the beach. He threw his cap, containing the insignia of the German Marine Infantry (with a swastika), on the sand, along with several other articles of clothing taken from the sea bag.

After Cullen left, Dasch and his group carried the boxes to the back of the beach and buried them in the sand. They buried the German uniforms that should have been sent back to the submarine with the sailors but had been left behind because of Cullen's surprise appearance. The four men left the beach and walked toward the highway. After wandering a bit in circles, they found railroad tracks and followed them to the station at Amagansett, arriving about 5 a.m. The station opened an hour and a half later. Dasch

2. Id. at 106.

bought four tickets for the 7:30 a.m. train to Jamaica. He attempted some light conversation with the station agent: "The fishing hasn't been very good out here, in fact it's been miserable because of the fog, and I guess we'll go home."[3]

The men arrived in Jamaica around nine in the morning. They split into two groups (Dasch with Burger, and Quirin with Heinck), bought some clothes, and got rid of some old clothing. After taking the train to Manhattan, they divided again: Dasch and Burger registering at the Hotel Governor Clinton, Heinck and Quirin at the Hotel Martinique. Later that afternoon, they met at the Horn & Hardart automat in Macy's department store and made plans to meet the following day at 1:00 at the Swiss Chalet restaurant on 52nd Street between Fifth and Sixth Avenues. If for some reason they failed to meet at the Swiss Chalet, they would meet that evening at 6:00 at Grant's Tomb at Riverside Drive and 121st Street.

On Saturday evening, Dasch and Burger ate dinner at the Coral Room in their hotel. According to their testimony before the military tribunal, they began to reveal to each other the depth of their opposition to the Nazi regime in Germany and their decision not to implement the sabotage plan. They went for a walk to Radio City, still confiding in each other. At the hotel, talking on the fourteenth floor with the window open, they teased that one might have to push the other out for disobeying orders. Burger said that he had smiled at Dasch and told him, "There was no reason for anyone going out the window and there was no reason to fight it out, because I felt very much the same way, and I could have told him the day before, the night before, that that was the idea."[4]

Dasch missed the meeting at the Swiss Chalet, but he and Burger reached Grant's Tomb about 6:20 p.m., just when Quirin and Heinck were about to leave. Neither side trusted the other. When Quirin and Heinck asked Dasch and Burger where they were staying, Dasch and Burger said the New Yorker. Quirin and Heinck were supposed to stay at the Chesterfield Hotel but had registered at

---

3. "Spy Not Clever, Coast Guard Says," New York Times, July 17, 1942, at 7.
4. Military Trial, at 2676.

the Martinque. Burger would later tell the tribunal, "There was no harmony. There was watching each other. It was no good; the spirit was not there."[5]

The four next planned to meet the following Tuesday at about 11 a.m. at the automat at Macy's. Unable to reach Dasch at the hotel, Burger was alone when he met with Quirin and Heinck, who said that they had left their hotel and moved to a rooming house at 149 West 76th. Quirin and Heinck were very suspicious about Dasch not showing up. Dasch did not appear because he had gone to a waiter's club he used to belong to and played pinochle Monday evening, all of Tuesday, and well into Wednesday morning. With Dasch dropping out of the picture, there was some talk of Quirin threatening to take command of the group. Dasch made it back to the hotel Wednesday morning, slept in, and made preparations to go to Washington, D.C., the next day. He made reservations at the Mayflower Hotel in Washington, checked out of the Governor Clinton, and caught the train at Pennsylvania Station on Thursday at 2:30 p.m., arriving in the nation's capital a little before 7 p.m.

Look What We Found

After Cullen returned to the Coast Guard station, he turned in the money and reported what had happened. Warren Barnes, the Chief Boatswain's Mate at the station, rushed over. Two members of the Coast Guard Intelligence, Lts. Sydney K. Franken and F. W. Nirschel, also drove to the station. When the Coast Guard returned to the beach area, Cullen found the package of German cigarettes left by Burger. They could see marks on the beach where something had been dragged. Over a hill, they spotted a place "that had been freshly dug up."[6] It was fairly easy to poke around and locate the boxes, buried about six inches under the sand. There were two boxes on the bottom and two on top. The sand on top was still wet.

5. Id. at 2632.
6. Id. at 127.

Within a few hours the sun would have dried that spot and made it more difficult to find the boxes.

The Coast Guard took the boxes back to the boat room at the station and opened one. Inside was a hermetically sealed tin containing time-bomb mechanisms and pens and pencils to be used as detonators. They brought the duffel bag in and emptied it, finding uniforms, civilian coats, and a fedora hat Dasch had worn. The collection included Burger's cap (with a swastika) and two shovels—one buried with the duffel bag, and the second left on the surface nearby. Other objects were discovered on top of the sand, including bathing trunks and a white canvas sneaker.

The Coast Guard put the four boxes and the other materials in a station wagon and drove to New York, to the Office of the Captain of the Port, John S. Baylis. There the other three boxes were opened. When they started to open the fourth box they heard a hissing sound. Out of an abundance of caution, they moved the box to the end of the pier. The noise had come from salt water touching the blocks of TNT.

At around noon, three FBI agents from the New York office arrived to look at the items and bring them to the office of Spencer J. Drayton. An FBI expert translated the German that appeared on some of the materials. An inventory of the collection disclosed a rich collection of fuses, blasting caps, match heads inside small brass tubular adapters, detonators with threaded ends, brass tubes closed at one end and threaded on the other, glass capsules containing sulfuric acid, the mechanical pen and pencil sets that functioned as time-delayed detonators, clocks used for the detonators, and metal buttons to set the firing pins on the clocks.

Also in the boxes were yellow demolition blocks that could be cut, drilled, or even dropped without fear of explosion. Fire would not cause explosion of the TNT. Even a rifle bullet would not set it off. The TNT blocks weighed about two pounds each, with a hole at one end to permit insertion of a detonator. One block could destroy steel rails or steel girders. About half a block would break a railroad rail. TNT blocks that looked like coals were covered with a plastic material. At the tribunal, FBI experts explained that detonators contained an explosive of sufficient power to set up a wave necessary to cause the TNT to explode, and safety fuses were like a "little powder train" to carry a flame to the material to be detonated. The powder burned about a foot every thirty seconds, allowing the saboteurs to reach safety.

Other mechanisms were explained at the tribunal. A charge of potassium chlorate and sugar would be ignited by coming in contact with sulfuric acid, producing a flash of flame. The body of the fountain pens, instead of containing an ink sack, held a capsule of sulfuric acid. At the end of the pen was a knob that, when turned, raised a small platform in the body of the pen and broke a capsule to release the acid. After the acid ate through a celluloid diaphragm, it came in contact with the chlorate and sugar. The flame was of sufficient intensity to set off the TNT blocks. By making adjustments, the explosion could be timed to go off after a set number of hours.

Another detonator relied on clockwork delay mechanisms. Extending from one edge of the clock was a notched wheel to wind the thirteen-jewel movement within. Also on the edge was a small lever to set the firing pin and a threaded hole into which the firing pin projected. A small indicator wheel showed the period of delay, up to fourteen days. The FBI performed a test, selecting the maximum delay, and it went off after fourteen days, three hours.[7]

Also introduced into evidence were the two handkerchiefs with secret writing on them. Dasch at first forgot the reagent used to make the writing visible but then recalled that it might be ammonia, which was correct. The FBI lab treated the handkerchief with ammonia, and the first word to appear in red was "Bingo," the German Intelligence name for Haupt. The other writing on Dasch's handkerchief was not very clear: a Lutheran minister in Rahway, New Jersey, Haupt's relative in Chicago, and the name of Helmut Leiner, who would know Kerling's location. There was also an address in Lisbon, where the two group leaders could contact Kappe. The writing on Kerling's handkerchief was much easier to read:

7. Id. at 234.

Maria da Conceico Lopez
Lisboa, Rua D. Carolo Mascarenhas 52 r/e dir

Pas Krepper c/o E. Frey
R.F.D. 2 Box 40 F, Rahway

Walter Froehling
3643 N. Whipple Str., Ch.

Ernest Dasch
11. Pelham Rd, N. London

F.D.P. (Franz Daniel Pastorius)

The address for Dasch's brother in New London, Connecticut, was fictitious, invented by Dasch to deceive Kappe. The last line, with initials, was to be used when contacting Pastor Krepper. Someone from the two groups would say "Franz Daniel," and he would answer "Pastorius." After an FBI chemist demonstrated to the tribunal how ammonia turned the hidden letters a dark red, a prosecutor asked the tribunal members if they could see. The president of the tribunal assured him, "The Commission can see and smell."[8]

Dasch Turns to the FBI

A news story in the *Washington Post* on July 22 suggests that Dasch, "unnerved by the mass of information collected by intelligence officers, made a statement so detailed and damning that it took the military commission two days to read it." Dasch indeed made a long statement, and the commission consumed much time in having it read, but the government knew little about the eight men and their whereabouts. The only solid evidence consisted of the boxes and other materials found at Amagansett. Otherwise, the FBI was looking for leads and hoping that some would show up.

In Germany, Burger had overheard a conversation about agents of the Gestapo infiltrating all parts of the FBI other than the headquar-

8. Id. at 758.

MISADVENTURES IN AMERICA 33

ters in Washington, D.C. Armed with this information, Dasch decided not to trust the FBI office in New York City; he would simply make an anonymous call to alert the New York office that they had landed, and then spill the beans to headquarters. Dasch thought that his story was so valuable that he would travel to Washington, D.C., and personally confide in FBI Director J. Edgar Hoover.

On Sunday evening, June 14, shortly before 8:00, Dasch called the New York office of the FBI and gave his name as Franz Daniel Pastorius. The agent on duty, Dean F. McWhorter, struggled with the spelling and put it down as "Frank Daniel Postorius." Dasch, insisting that a record be made of the call, said that he had arrived from Germany two days ago. After refusing to come to the FBI office or reveal his address in New York City, he told the agent that he was going to Washington, D.C., on either Thursday or Friday to talk to Director J. Edgar Hoover "or his secretary." In making a record of this call, McWhorter added this as his last line: "This memo is being prepared only for the purpose of recording the call made by POSTORIUS."[9] His notation appears to assign a low priority to the information, even though by Sunday evening the FBI in New York City (and Washington) knew of the boxes uncovered at Amagansett. There is no evidence that either McWhorter or his superiors notified Washington about the call.

Why Dasch waited another five days to reveal the sabotage plan to the FBI in Washington has never been adequately explained. He and Burger insisted that the immersion with card playing had been needed to settle Dasch's nerves and clear his head. Dasch offers other reasons in his book, saying that there "was no real need for hurry since I had the mission completely under control."[10] That might have been true of his foursome, but not Kerling's. Dasch also spoke of his plan "to wait a few days to give Haupt a chance to show his colors too" (by turning himself in).[11] That does not make sense either. If Dasch took almost a week to

9. Id. at 2583.
10. Dasch, Eight Spies Against America, at 109.
11. Id. at 114.

contact the FBI in Washington, why not give Haupt, who arrived in Florida four days after Dasch's team reached Amagansett, an equal amount of time?

In any event, Dasch reached the Mayflower Hotel Thursday evening and went out for dinner. At the restaurant, he recognized a waiter, Louis Martin, he had known in previous years. Later they went out for a few drinks. When Dasch asked who he should see in Washington on law enforcement matters, Martin suggested Attorney General Francis Biddle. Dasch dutifully wrote the name down in his address book. Some weeks later he would indeed see Biddle, but not in the Attorney General's office. It would be at the military tribunal.

On Friday morning, Dasch called the Information Service of the federal government to find out who to call about military espionage: the Secret Service or the FBI? The operator advised him to call the Adjutant General's office. Dasch talked to the secretary of Col. H. F. Kramer, who was not in, and said that he had landed with a group from Germany. He asked her to have Kramer call him back when he returned. Dasch then called the FBI and talked with agent Duane L. Traynor, who asked him to come over at 11 a.m. Dasch wanted to come earlier, and they agreed on 10:30. After Dasch expressed uncertainty about how to get to Traynor's office, Traynor sent several agents to pick Dasch up and escort him back to Room 2250 of the Justice Department building. After the conversation with Traynor, Kramer reached Dasch by phone, and Dasch told him that he was on his way over to the FBI.

Traynor was somewhat skeptical about Dasch's story. At one point, according to Dasch's testimony, he said, "'You know, George, when you came to my office here, I didn't believe you; I thought you were a crackpot—clown'; something like that—'I just didn't believe you. Then finally when you opened up—then I knew we had something, after all.'"[12] Part of the "opening up" occurred when Dasch unlocked his briefcase and showed the agents the contents: $82,550 in $50 bills.

12. Military Trial, at 2542.

Kerling's Group Lands at Ponte Vedra

About three or four days before the second submarine reached Florida, Neubauer defied instructions about trying to contact his family or friends and wrote a letter to his wife, telling her to get on a Swedish boat that was taking American citizens to the United States. He showed it to Kerling, who thought that it was all right to send. Neubauer had to get one of the crew to ignore orders by promising to mail the letter.

The submarine reached Ponte Vedra, near Jacksonville, Florida, on the evening of June 16. After midnight, the sub approached the shore and brought the men safely to the beach without incident. The men returned their uniforms to the sub, buried the boxes, and walked along the beach for an hour or two. After arriving at Jacksonville Beach in their swimming suits, they waited until about 11 a.m. and changed into their civilian clothes to catch a bus to Jacksonville, arriving about noon on Wednesday, June 17.

As with the group in New York City, Kerling's team broke into two pairs. Kerling and Neubauer stayed together, registering at the Seminole Hotel as Edward J. Kelly and Henry Nicholas. Thiel and Haupt checked into a different hotel under the names William Thomas and Herbert Haupt. That evening, it was agreed that Thiel and Haupt would catch a train the next morning to Cincinnati. Thiel stayed there a short time while Haupt continued on to Chicago. Kerling and Neubauer also took a train to Cincinnati. As they passed factories and railroads, they could see how well they were guarded. The two seemed to agree that there was little chance of successfully carrying out their orders. In Cincinnati, they split up—Kerling going to New York City (with Thiel), and Neubauer traveling to Chicago.

Haupt arrived in Chicago about 3 p.m. on Friday, June 19, and took a taxi to see his uncle, Walter Froehling. He planned to tell his uncle that Walter's brother Otto was being held in a concentration camp but would be released if Walter agreed to let his house be used as a mail drop. Whether Haupt actually told his uncle that story is uncertain. When he reached the Froehling home, Walter called

Haupt's mother and drove over to pick her up. Haupt's father arrived somewhat later, about 7 p.m. Haupt gave Walter a zipper bag with $15,000 to $20,000 in a false bottom and asked him to hide it "on top of the mantel in the dining-room."[13] Everyone knew that Haupt had come to America in a submarine with three others, but they did not know exactly what the men planned to do. Obviously, he was acting as an agent for the German government. They advised him to register for the draft to "be here legally."[14]

On Sunday, Haupt met Neubauer in Chicago. On Tuesday, after being warned by his mother that the FBI had been asking questions, Haupt registered for the draft and stopped by the FBI office to inform the bureau that he had returned from Mexico. Something about the visit and Haupt's story made the FBI suspicious; when Haupt left the FBI office, he was followed each day until his arrest on June 27. In the meantime, Haupt went to Simpson Optical with his parents and learned that he could start work there beginning Thursday.

On Tuesday, June 23, Haupt bought a used 1941 Pontiac sport coupe for $1,045, putting it in his father's name in case he was arrested. He took $400 from his money belt to use as the down payment, hiding the rest of the money (about $2,500) under the rug in his parents' bedroom. He told his father where the money was. He tore up the draft card given to him in Germany, with the name of Larry Jordan, and burned it in the kitchen.[15] Gerda Stuckmann came over, and they talked about getting married. He gave her $10 for the blood test. On Thursday, he drove out in the country with his parents' friends. They had the impression of being followed.

William Wernecke, a friend of Herbert Haupt, suggested some techniques for avoiding the draft. Bill had faked all kinds of illnesses, including rheumatism, to receive a deferment. He advised Haupt to take three nitroglycerin pills before having an electrocardiogram, to throw the results off, and also to give $100 to a "church"

13. Id. at 1644.
14. Id. at 1646.
15. Id. at 1651.

that would register him as a Bible student dating back to 1941. Haupt did not pursue the latter option, but he did take the nitroglycerin pills and have an electrocardiogram. He was unable to pick up the results, however, because the FBI picked him up first.

Haupt also met with Otto Wergin and his wife, letting them know that he had arrived by submarine from Germany. Mr. Wergin offered to help Haupt with his sabotage mission. The Wergins were close friends of the Haupts, and their son, Wolfgang, had traveled with Herbert the previous year from Chicago to Mexico, then by ship to Japan, and finally to Germany. Haupt said that Kappe, in Germany, had threatened (at least by implication) to pick up Wolfgang and put him in a concentration camp if Haupt refused to participate in the sabotage plan.

Kerling and Neubauer waited a day and took a train to Cincinnati on Friday morning. Neubauer went on to Chicago, reaching there on Sunday, June 21, at seven in the morning. He registered at the LaSalle Hotel and met Haupt at the Chicago Theatre. On Monday or Tuesday night, Neubauer visited the home of Harry and Emma Jaques, friends of his wife. He asked them to keep $3,600 for him, and they agreed. After Mrs. Jaques mentioned receiving a letter from Mrs. Kerling, Neubauer disclosed that Kerling had come over on the same sub. Mr. Jaques said that he did not want to hear anymore about Neubauer's plans or intentions.[16] Neubauer returned to the Jaques home on Friday night, about 10 p.m., to talk some more. They had heard over the radio that German agents had landed by submarine in the United States. They asked whether he wanted any of the money, and he said no. Neubauer, increasingly nervous about the sabotage mission, kept switching hotels. On Wednesday, June 24, he left the LaSalle and checked in at the Sherman Hotel. On Friday, he moved again, this time choosing the Sheridan Plaza Hotel.

Kerling, having accompanied Neubauer to Cincinnati, met up with Thiel, and the two of them took a train to New York City. They arrived on Sunday, June 21, and registered at the Commodore

16. Id. at 1747.

Hotel. On June 22, they took an afternoon subway to Astoria to see Helmut Leiner, a friend of Kerling. Thiel went up to the front porch and brought Leiner down the street to talk with Kerling. Later, over drinks, Thiel asked Leiner to find his friend Anthony Cramer. Thiel had known Cramer in Detroit, Hammond, and New York City. On June 23, Thiel met Cramer at the information booth of Grand Central Station and told him that he had just come over by submarine. He asked Cramer to place $3,500 in cash in a safe deposit box in a bank, and Cramer agreed.

When Kerling reached New York City, he wanted to see his wife and his girlfriend, Hedwig Engemann. He thought of getting a place out in the country with Hedy. One possible plan was to go to Florida with Hedy (perhaps in the car bought by Haupt), retrieve the explosives, and store the boxes at the place in the country. He saw Hedy at Central Park on Monday afternoon for about half an hour and also the next day. She knew that he had come back by submarine. He asked her to go with him to Cincinnati, Chicago, and Florida, and she agreed. On Tuesday evening, June 23, Kerling planned to meet his wife at the Shelton Hotel on Lexington and 49th Street; Helmut Leiner had arranged the meeting. But before Kerling could see her, the FBI closed in.

A Quick Roundup

News of the saboteurs' dramatic capture splashed across the headlines on June 28. Announced the *New York Times:* FBI SEIZES 8 SAB-OTEURS LANDED BY U-BOATS HERE AND IN FLORIDA TO BLOW UP WAR PLANTS. The article gave full credit to the FBI: "Despite their training the two gangs of four men each fell afoul of special agents of the Federal Bureau of Investigation."[17] The *Times* mentioned the encounter with the Coast Guardsman at Amagansett, but the task of apprehending all eight men appeared to be solely the work of the FBI: "before the men could begin carrying out their orders the FBI

17. "Invaders Confess," New York Times, June 28, 1942, at 1.

was on their trail and the roundup began. One after another they fell into the special agents' net."[18] Other newspaper accounts gloried in the FBI's detection abilities: "Almost from the moment the first group set foot on United States soil the special agents of the Federal Bureau of Investigation were on their trail."[19] The FBI seized the men "almost as they landed on the sandy beaches."[20] A *Washington Post* editorial gushed at the FBI's "brilliant job of detection."[21]

Attorney General Biddle's memoirs, published long after the country was aware that Dasch had turned in his colleagues, repeated the fiction of FBI omniscience. He claimed that the agency "was on the job in a few minutes" and that "it was generally concluded that a particularly brilliant FBI agent, probably attending the school in sabotage where the eight had been trained, had been able to get on the inside, and make regular reports to America."[22] One of Roosevelt's aides, William Hassett, talked about the infighting among federal agencies, clamoring for recognition. A Secret Service agent was "plenty sore because Hoover's boys hogged all the credit for running down the culprits."[23]

Hoover did not acknowledge the assistance from the Coast Guard. When reporters pressed for the "Coast Guard side," they were told that there was "no Coast Guard side—for publication."[24] The FBI continued to be the sole spokesman for the Administration. Although the Coast Guard refused to confirm that Cullen had been unarmed, photographs afterward showed two Guardsmen patrolling the beaches of Amagansett with rifles.[25] Lewis Wood of the *New York Times* wrote a lengthy story about Cullen's encounter with

18. Id. at 30.
19. Id.
20. "Nazi Saboteurs Face Stern Army Justice," New York Times, July 5, 1942, at 6E.
21. "FBI's Master Stroke," Washington Post, June 29, 1942, at 6.
22. Francis Biddle, In Brief Authority 326, 328 (Garden City, N.Y.: Doubleday, 1962).
23. William D. Hassett, Off the Record with F.D.R., 1942–1945, at 74 (New Brunswick, N.J.: Rutgers University Press, 1958).
24. "Saboteurs Face Military Justice; Inquiry Widens," New York Times, June 30, 1942, at 6.
25. Id.

Dasch and provided verbatim details of their conversation. Wood explained that his story did not violate the rules of secrecy imposed by the tribunal because he had relied on Coast Guard files assembled before the trial.[26]

Some reporters were getting close to the truth about Dasch's role. On July 5, the *Washington Post* reported that one of the Germans had "lost his nerve" and had given a Coast Guardsman "hot money" that made it easy for federal agents to stay on their trail.[27] This particular incident was not yet linked to Dasch. A day later, however, the *Post* learned that Dasch might stand a chance of clemency because he had cooperated with U.S. officials "in procuring evidence against the others."[28] Another *Post* story on July 8 reported that Dasch would have his own counsel, Col. Carl L. Ristine, and was likely to escape the death penalty.[29] On July 16, the *Post* stated that on the previous day the military trial had been consumed by reading the confession of one of the men who was an "informer."[30] The reporter connected that person to Dasch.

Dasch made it easy for the FBI to round up the other three members of his group in New York City. He gave FBI agents Burger's room number at the Hotel Governor Clinton; through Burger, the FBI could learn the whereabouts of Quirin and Heinck. On Saturday, June 20, Burger left the hotel about 3 p.m. and went to a Rogers Peet store to pick up some clothing. He, Quirin, and Heinck had bought clothes there earlier in the week and planned to meet at the store. Burger returned to the Clinton and left his door unlocked. When FBI agents entered his room at 5 p.m., he seemed to be expecting them.[31]

26. "Lone Coast Guardsman Put FBI on Trail of Saboteurs," New York Times, July 16, 1942, at 1, 38.

27. "German Spy's Loss of Nerve Led to Capture," Washington Post, July 5, 1942, at 11.

28. "Saboteurs' Trial to Start in Washington Wednesday," Washington Post, July 6, 1942, at 1.

29. "One Spy Gets Separate Counsel, Hinting at Leniency for Him," Washington Post, July 8, 1942, at 1.

30. "Confession of Spy Who Told All Read to Military Commission," Washington Post, July 16, 1942, at 7.

31. Military Trial, at 453–54.

Quirin and Heinck, followed by the FBI after leaving Rogers Peet, took a bus uptown to 72nd and Broadway and began walking to their rooming house. Quirin, who had gone ahead, was picked up by the FBI about 5 p.m. Heinck had stopped to make purchases at several stores. When he emerged from a delicatessen, he was taken into custody at 5:15 p.m. He later told the FBI that he had had a "funny dream" of Dasch standing in the FBI office and telling them "about everything." Heinck had learned that Dasch had told the Coast Guardsman that "he will hear from Washington, or something like that; and that made me suspicious."[32]

Locating the other four men was not as simple. Dasch told the FBI that he would be meeting Kerling in Cincinnati on July 4, between noon and 2 p.m., in the grill of the Hotel Gibson. The FBI did not want to wait that long, for fear that some sabotage operations might be attempted. On June 23, in New York City, Kerling met Leiner for dinner, and Leiner called Kerling's wife at her workplace to arrange a meeting that same evening at the Shelton Hotel. After dinner, Kerling left Leiner and met Thiel at the corner of Lexington and 44th. Thiel was with an individual he introduced as "Tony" (Anthony Cramer). Kerling left them to meet his wife but was arrested by the FBI at 10 p.m. in front of the Shelton Hotel. A search of his room at the Commodore Hotel disclosed two pieces of luggage with false bottoms. One contained $24,850 in $50 bills, and the other $29,700 in $50 bills. Kerling's money belt had $3,700 in $50 bills.

Shortly after picking up Kerling, the FBI apprehended Thiel between 11:30 and 11:50 p.m., a few feet west of the entrance to the Commodore Hotel on 42nd Street. Thiel's wallet contained $554.06 in cash, his Social Security card, and a draft registration certificate for selective service. The cards carried the name of William Thomas.

The FBI took Kerling to Jacksonville to look for the explosives buried on the beach. After walking along the beach in an effort to locate some landmarks, particularly three palm stumps, Kerling

32. Id. at 2447–48.

found the spot. The boxes contained much the same materials as those buried on the beach at Amagansett. Kerling refused to disclose the location of another burial place containing German Marine caps and shovels. The FBI had to return a second time to retrieve those materials. Using iron bars, the agents probed the sand for several hours before locating the buried items.[33]

Haupt's mother had told him that the FBI had been to her house asking questions about his draft status. Taking the bull by the horns, Haupt went to the FBI office in Chicago and said that he had been out of the country, in Mexico. His story did not sound quite right, and the FBI put a tail on him. He was apprehended a little after 9 a.m. on June 27, on Webster Street, at the elevated station just off Cissell Street. The FBI arrested Neubauer on June 27 at his room in the Sheridan Plaza. When Haupt was picked up, he said that he "knew all the time that Peter Burger would turn us in, because he had been in a concentration camp and had told me about the horrors he suffered and the horrors he had seen other people suffer in the concentration camp in Germany." Haupt knew that Burger hated the Gestapo "more than anything else on earth, that his wife lost a child because of the treatments of her by them."[34]

33. Leon O. Prior, "Nazi Invasion of Florida," 49 Florida Historical Quarterly 129, 136–37 (October 1970).

34. Military Trial, at 1997.

3

The Military Tribunal at Work

Throughout the long days of interrogation, FBI agents assumed that the eight Germans would be arraigned before a district judge and tried in civil court. The agents encouraged Dasch to go before a judge and plead guilty. In none of those discussions did the agents consider the prospect of a military tribunal, a procedure last used during the Civil War.1 The conduct of the trial against those who conspired to assassinate President Abraham Lincoln, followed by the public hanging of four (including Mary Surratt), marked a sour chapter in American judicial proceedings. Military tribunals seemed an unlikely precedent to revive. However, after news of the FBI captures reached the newspapers on June 28, several members of Congress advocated military rather than civil prosecution.2 Administration officials also closely analyzed the military option.

The Milligan *Hurdle*

To prosecute the German saboteurs by military tribunal, the Administration had to surmount the Civil War case of *Ex parte Milligan*

---

1. For analyses of military tribunals during the Civil War, see Mark E. Neely, Jr., The Fate of Liberty: Abraham Lincoln and Civil Liberties 160–84 (New York: Oxford University Press, 1991); William Hanchett, The Lincoln Murder Conspiracies (Urbana: University of Illinois Press, 1983); and Lewis L. Laska & James M. Smith, "'Hell and the Devil': Andersonville and the Trial of Captain Henry Wirz, C.S.A., 1865," 68 Military Law Review 77 (1975).

2. Two Senators making that recommendation were Joseph O'Mahoney of Wyoming and Patrick A. McCarran of Nevada. "Spy Aides in City Captured by FBI; More Are Hunted," New York Times, June 29, 1942, at 4.

(1866). In 1864 the military had arrested Lambdin P. Milligan, a
U.S. citizen from Indiana, on charges of conspiracy. Found guilty
before a military commission, he was sentenced to be hanged. He
presented a petition of habeas corpus to the federal courts, asking to
be discharged from unlawful imprisonment because the military
had no jurisdiction over him. He insisted that he was entitled to trial
by jury in a civilian court.

The question was whether President Lincoln, in times of emergency, could suspend the writ of habeas corpus and declare martial
law. That issue had been ruled on in 1861 by Chief Justice Roger
Taney, sitting as a circuit judge in Baltimore. He concluded that
Lincoln had no power to suspend the writ and that a prisoner held
by the military—John Merryman—should be set free. However,
when Taney attempted to serve a paper at the prison where Merryman was held, prison officials refused to let Taney's marshal carry
out his duty. Taney, sidestepping a political collision he could not
win, acquiesced with these words:

I have exercised all the power which the constitution and laws confer upon
me, but that power has been resisted by a force too strong for me to overcome. . . . I shall, therefore, order all the proceedings in this case, with my
opinion, to be filed and recorded in the circuit court of the United States for
the district court of Maryland, and direct the clerk to transmit a copy, under
seal, to the president of the United States. It will then remain for that high
officer, in fulfillment of his constitutional obligation to "take care that the
laws be faithfully executed," to determine what measures he will take to
cause the civil process of the United States to be respected and enforced.[3]

Only with the war over and Lincoln in his grave did the Court
breathe some life into the privilege of the writ of habeas corpus. In
the case of Lambdin Milligan, the Court held that military courts
could not function in states where federal courts were open and operating.[4] Although this decision is generally praised today as one of
the great landmarks in defense of civil liberties, it was not so popular when issued. Critics charged that the Court had thrown its

3. Ex parte Merryman, 17 Fed. Case No. 9,487 (1861), at 153.
4. Ex parte Milligan, 71 U.S. (4 Wall.) 2 (1866).

weight against those in the North who intended to carry out a program of Reconstruction in the South. Numerous newspapers compared the decision to the *Dred Scott* case.[5]

Instead of delivering a unanimous opinion, which was possible and would have minimized criticism, five members of the Court decided not only to rule in favor of Milligan but also to hold more broadly that the military commission in Indiana was not authorized by Congress, nor was it in the power of Congress to authorize it. On that point, four Justices broke away and dissented. The division within the Court invited criticism that the ruling was "not a judicial opinion; it is a political act."[6]

In response to *Milligan,* Congress passed legislation to limit the Court's jurisdiction to hear cases involving martial law and military trials. Although cases were already pending with regard to the conduct of U.S. officials during and immediately after the war, Congress gave indemnity to all officials who had implemented presidential proclamations from March 4, 1861, to June 30, 1866, with respect to martial law and military trials. The statute provided: "And no civil court of the United States, or of any State, or of the District of Columbia, or of any district or territory of the United States, shall have or take jurisdiction of, or in any manner reverse any of the proceedings had or acts done as aforesaid."[7]

あforいsaid: 所述 の

Interdepartmental Conflicts

FBI plea bargaining with Dasch might have prompted the Administration to propose a military tribunal. Confessions from suspects are supposed to be given voluntarily, without any promise or inducement from the government. Yet Dasch had been told by FBI agents that if he agreed to plead guilty, they would set in motion the wheels for a presidential pardon. At the military trial, Dasch's attorney

5. Charles Warren, The Supreme Court in United States History 2:428–32 (Boston: Little Brown, 1937).
6. Id. at 432.
7. 14 Stat. 432, 433 (1867).

propose a military tribunal,
m civil

plen: 调解   withdraw 撤回了

divulge 暴露了

asked one of the FBI agents: "Was it stated as a part of that proposal that after his plea of guilty he should be sentenced and that during the trial he should not divulge anything with respect to the agreement that was made, and that after the case had died down and for about, say, three to six months, the F.B.I. would get a Presidential pardon for him?" The agent replied: "That, in substance, is true."[8] The FBI warned Dasch that if he appeared in open court to testify about cooperating with the government, it might endanger his family in Germany.[9]

On Saturday afternoon, June 27, the FBI told Dasch that he would be indicted and tried before a civil court. In testimony, Dasch said that he agreed to plead guilty with the understanding that everything would be kept quiet. Yet the following morning, he looked through the slit in his cell door and saw an agent reading the Sunday newspaper with Dasch's photo "in front."[10] Believing that he had been betrayed, Dasch withdrew his offer to plead guilty. He now wanted to go into civil court and make a full explanation, even if it put his family at risk.[11]

This turn of events helped convince the Administration to choose a military trial and prohibit any appeals to civil courts. The public had the impression that uncanny FBI organizational skills had quickly uncovered the plot. FBI Director J. Edgar Hoover, after being praised for discovering the saboteurs, did not want it known that one of them had turned himself in and fingered the others. Neither did President Franklin D. Roosevelt and other top officials. The government did not want to broadcast how easily German U-boats had reached American shores undetected. By sending a message that the executive branch had a vast capacity to intercept enemy saboteurs, the United States might discourage future attempts by Germany.

There was a second reason for a military trial. The statute on sabotage carried a maximum thirty-year penalty, and even on that

8. Military Trial, at 541.
9. Id. at 541, 548.
10. Id. at 2546.
11. Id. at 677.

uncanny: 超乎人的

1. avoiding to defend   making a full explana

charge, the government had little confidence that it could prevail. The men had not actually committed an act of sabotage. In his memoirs, Attorney General Francis Biddle concluded that an indictment for attempted sabotage probably would not have been sustained in a civil court "on the ground that the preparations and landings were not close enough to the planned act of sabotage to constitute attempt." He pointed out that if a man bought a pistol, with the intent to murder someone, "that is not an attempt at murder."[12] The prosecution could cite federal law on conspiracy to commit crimes, but the maximum penalty was only three years.[13] A military court offered many advantages: it could act in secret, move swiftly, and mete out the ultimate penalty. There was some debate within the Administration whether Burger and Haupt, as naturalized U.S. citizens, would have to be tried in civil court, but plans were soon under way to prosecute all eight in a military trial.

Maj. Gen. Myron C. Cramer, Judge Advocate General of the Army, had similar concerns about the relatively light penalties available in civil proceedings. In a memo of June 28, he said that a district court "would be unable to impose an adequate sentence." It could impose a sentence of two years and a fine of $10,000 for conspiracy to commit a crime. The government could also punish the Germans for violating immigration laws by entering the country clandestinely and for violating customs laws by bringing the articles they had carried ashore. However, Cramer concluded that the "maximum permissible punishment for these offenses would be less than it is desirable to impose."[14] Oscar Cox, in the Solicitor General's office, knew of Cramer's estimate that what the Germans had done was "only a two-year offense at most."[15]

12. Biddle, In Brief Authority, at 328.
13. Id.
14. Memorandum for the Assistant Chief of Staff, G-2, June 28, 1942, by Maj. Gen. Myron C. Cramer, at 4, in "German Saboteurs" file, RG 107, Office of the Secretary of War, Stimson "Safe Files," National Archives, College Park, Md.
15. Memo of June 29, 1942, Sunday, "German Saboteurs," Papers of Oscar Cox, Diaries and Related Material, Box 146, FDR Library.

Late Sunday afternoon, June 28, Secretary of War Henry L. Stimson received a phone call from Biddle, scheduling a meeting the next day to decide whether to prosecute the saboteurs in civil court or military court.[16] At about noon on Monday, Biddle told Stimson the result of conferences that Biddle had been having with Cramer. To Stimson's surprise, Biddle, "instead of straining every nerve to retain civil jurisdiction of these saboteurs, was quite ready to turn them over to a military court." Biddle suggested that instead of a court-martial the government should appoint a special military commission, with Stimson serving as chairman. Stimson thought it was not "seemly" for him to both appoint the commission and chair it, so he recommended that a civilian chair the commission. However, the person he had in mind, Robert Patterson, preferred that the court be wholly military.[17]

The press got wind of these meetings. On June 29, Biddle indicated that the eight Germans might be prosecuted by the War Department and that Biddle had been consulting with Stimson and Cramer.[18] A press release by the Justice Department on June 30 disclosed that Biddle and his staff "have been in constant consultation throughout the day with the Secretary of War, the Judge Advocate General, and other War Department officials."[19]

Oscar Cox sent a memo to Biddle on June 29, concluding that the men could be tried by either a general court-martial or a military tribunal. *Ex parte Milligan,* Cox said, did not require a civil trial for enemy aliens who came through the lines out of uniform for the purpose of committing sabotage. In comparing the merits of the two types of military courts, he emphasized that a general court-martial "must follow statutory procedures presented in the Articles of War," whereas the procedures of a military commission are not necessarily governed by statutes. Yet he added this qualifi-

16. Diary of Henry L. Stimson, June 28, 1942, Roll 7, at 128–29, LC (hereafter Stimson Diary).

17. Id., June 29, 1942, at 131.

18. "Saboteurs Face Military Justice; Inquiry Widens," New York Times, June 30, 1942, at 1.

19. Press Release, Department of Justice, June 30, 1942, "German Saboteurs, Trial of (I)," Papers of Oscar Cox, Box 61, FDR Library.

cation: "it has been the practice for military commissions to follow the composition and procedure of courts-martial."[20] The military tribunal created by President Roosevelt would devise its own procedures, departing from court-martial practice whenever it chose to.

By June 30, journalists learned that the basic decision to proceed by military trial had been made.[21] Stimson spent that day selecting people to serve on the commission.[22] Biddle received a note from Roosevelt on June 30, stating that it was his inclination to try all eight by court-martial. Roosevelt regarded the death penalty as "almost obligatory."[23] He said that "without splitting hairs" he could see no difference between this case and the hanging of Major André during the Revolutionary War, adding this warning: "i.e., don't split hairs, Mr. Attorney General."[24] All that remained was the official announcement. On July 1, the word was just about out. Newspaper stories stated that Roosevelt would appoint a seven-member military commission to try the eight men, and that Biddle would share prosecutorial duties with Cramer. Reporters assumed that the trial would take place at a military site.[25] On that guess they erred.

Other factors played into the creation of a military tribunal. To Stimson, the "main problem" was whether Biddle should take part in the trial. He saw little reason for the Attorney General to commit time and energy to a case "of such little national importance." Surely Biddle had more important duties in heading the Justice Department and could find people with the requisite competence and experience to conduct the prosecution. However, as Stimson noted in his diary on July 1, Biddle "seemed to have the bug of publicity in his mind."[26] That he did.

20. Memo from Cox to Biddle, June 29, 1942, id. at 3.

21. "Army to Try 8 Saboteurs Landed by Sub," Washington Post, June 30, 1942, at 1.

22. Stimson Diary, June 30, 1942, at 133.

23. Memo from Roosevelt to Biddle, June 30, 1942, PSF, "Departmental File, Justice, 1940–44," Box 56, FDR Library.

24. Biddle, In Brief Authority, at 330.

25. "Death to Be Sought for 8 Saboteurs," Washington Post, July 2, 1942, at 12.

26. Stimson Diary, July 1, 1942, at 136.

Roosevelt's Proclamation

A memo from Biddle to Roosevelt on June 30 set forth the main elements of trial by military commission. The advantages were swiftness and the ability to impose the death penalty. Espionage laws and treason carried the death penalty, but Biddle explained why it would be difficult to prove either charge in court. As to the possibility of review by civil courts, Biddle recommended language to deny the eight Germans such access. He believed that his proposed language would not represent a suspension of the writ of habeas corpus, although the wording "should produce the same practical result for such enemies." By confining the language to the eight Germans, he thought that the Administration "would not raise the broad policy questions which would follow a 'suspension' of the writ." It had "long been traditional," he said, "to deny our enemies access to the courts in time of war."[27]

On July 2, less than a week after the eight men had been apprehended, President Roosevelt issued Proclamation 2561 to create a military tribunal. The proclamation carried this title: "Denying Certain Enemies Access to the Courts of the United States."[28] The initial paragraph began by stating that the "safety of the United States demands that all enemies who have entered upon the territory of the United States as part of an invasion or predatory incursion, or who have entered in order to commit sabotage, espionage, or other hostile or warlike acts, should be promptly tried in accordance with the law of war."

Reference to the "law of war" was crucial. Had Roosevelt cited the "Articles of War," he would have triggered the statutory procedures established by Congress for courts-martial. The category "law of war," undefined by statute, represents a more diffuse collection

27. Memo from Biddle to Roosevelt, June 30, 1942, OF 5036, Box 4, FDR Library. A memo by the Justice Department on July 1 explored the risk of the eight saboteurs seeking a writ of habeas corpus. Memo from Ernest W. Jennes to Oscar Cox, July 1, 1942, "German Saboteurs, Trial of (I)," Papers of Oscar Cox, Box 61, FDR Library.
28. 7 Fed. Reg. 5101 (1942).

1. law of War

of principles and customs developed in the field of international law.[29] A military tribunal could thus pick and choose among the principles and procedures that it found compatible with the overall theme of Roosevelt's proclamation.

The second paragraph of the proclamation described Roosevelt acting as "President of the United States of America and Commander in Chief of the Army and Navy of the United States, by virtue of the authority vested in me by the Constitution and the statutes of the United States." Thus, Roosevelt was not claiming inherent or exclusive constitutional authority. He acted under a mix of constitutional authority accorded to the President and statutory authority granted by Congress. The document goes on to proclaim "that all persons who are subjects, citizens or residents of any nation at war with the United States or who give obedience to or act under the direction of any such nation, and who during time of war enter or attempt to enter the United States or any territory or possession thereof, through coastal or boundary defenses, and are charged with committing or attempting or preparing to commit sabotage, espionage, hostile or warlike acts, or violations of the law of war, shall be subject to the law of war and to the jurisdiction of military tribunals."

The second paragraph contained a controversial provision that denied the eight men access to any civil court: "such persons shall not be privileged to seek any remedy or maintain any proceeding directly or indirectly, or to have any such remedy or proceeding sought on their behalf, in the courts of the United States, or of its States, territories, and possessions, except under such regulations as the Attorney General, with the approval of the Secretary of War, may from time to time prescribe." Roosevelt felt strongly about denying judicial review to the saboteurs. He told Biddle, "I won't

29. In 10 U.S.C. § 821 (2000), Congress takes notice of the law of war in this manner: "The provisions of this chapter conferring jurisdiction upon courts-martial do not deprive military commissions, provost courts, or other military tribunals of concurrent jurisdiction with respect to offenders or offenses that by statute or by the law of war may be tried by military commissions, provost courts, or other military tribunals."

deny access to civil cony
→ no vigh

give them up. . . . I won't hand them over to any United States marshal armed with a writ of habeas corpus. Understand?"[30]

Also on July 2, Roosevelt issued a military order appointing the members of the military commission, the prosecutors, and the defense counsel.[31] Acting under the 38th Article of War, he appointed Maj. Gen. Frank R. McCoy to serve as president of the commission and appointed three Major Generals and three Brigadier Generals to complete the seven-man tribunal. The military order directed Biddle and Cramer to conduct the prosecution. It is extremely unusual for an Attorney General to prosecute a case, but Biddle urged Roosevelt to appoint him the prosecuting official before the commission. With Secretary Stimson opposed, the Administration reached a compromise by having Biddle and Cramer share the task. The military order assigned Col. Cassius M. Dowell and Col. Kenneth Royall to serve as defense counsel. Dowell had forty years of military service. Royall, a Harvard Law School graduate with extensive experience as a trial lawyer, would conduct most of the defense before the commission and the Supreme Court. On July 7, Col. Carl L. Ristine was appointed to represent Dasch, leaving Dowell and Royall to defend the other seven.

In directing the commission to meet on July 8, "or as soon thereafter as is practicable," the order referred to the trying of offenses against both the "law of war and the Articles of War." However, the order clearly liberated the commission from some of the restrictions established by Congress in the Articles of War. The commission would "have power to and shall, as occasion requires, make such rules for the conduct of the proceeding, consistent with the powers of military commissions under the Articles of War, as it shall deem necessary for a full and fair trial of the matters before it." The power to "make such rules" freed the commission from procedures enacted by Congress and the *Manual for Courts-Martial*. Thus, the commission could admit evidence "as would, in the opinion of the President of the Commission, have probative

30. Biddle, In Brief Authority, at 331.
31. 7 Fed. Reg. 5103 (1942).

value to a reasonable man." The meaning of the reasonable-man test would be worked out over the course of the trial as the commission issued its rulings.

The military order plainly departed from the Articles of War with regard to the votes needed for sentencing. The order stated that the concurrence of "at least two-thirds of the members of the Commission present shall be necessary for a conviction or sentence." Two-thirds of the commission could convict and sentence the men to death. Under a court-martial, a death penalty required a unanimous vote.

Finally, Roosevelt's order directed that the trial record, including any judgment or sentence, be transmitted "directly to me for my action thereon." This, too, marked a significant departure from military trials. Under Articles of War 46 and 50½, any conviction or sentence by a military court was subject to review within the military system, including the Judge Advocate General's office. The July 2 order vested the "final reviewing authority" in Roosevelt.

Issues with the Media

The trial took place on the west wing of the fifth floor of the Justice Department building, in Room 5235, used in the past as a lecture hall. To preserve secrecy, the windows were covered with heavy black curtains, and the glass doors at each end of the corridor were blacked over. Soldiers patrolled outside the room to prevent entrance except by authorized parties. The public and the press were excluded.

Elmer Davis, director of the Office of War Information, favored an "open policy" in the dissemination of news about the trial and even wanted some newspaper witnesses at the trial. Initially, Roosevelt seemed to support having three witnesses present, one from each of the news services.[32] Stimson, annoyed that Biddle had been talking to Roosevelt "behind my back," told Roosevelt on July

32. Stimson Diary, July 6, 1942, at 144–45.

6 that it would be "extremely dangerous" to allow the press in "at any stage of the taking of the evidence because there were certain matters which would necessarily come out which ought not to be in the hands of anybody outside the officials of the trial."[33] As a compromise, Roosevelt suggested that the trial begin with three witnesses but that when the Judge Advocate General rose to present his case and outline the evidence, he should ask the court to close the proceedings.[34]

Rules adopted by the tribunal on July 7 flatly stated that "sessions shall not be open to the public."[35] An announcement followed the next day: "The sessions will be closed, necessarily so, due to the nature of the testimony, which involves the security of the United States and the lives of its soldiers, sailors and citizens."[36] With the permission of General McCoy, Biddle and Cramer drafted a statement on "the reasons for employing a military commission and the reasons for secrecy" in the trial of the eight Germans. It was "of the utmost importance that no information be permitted to reach the enemy on any of these matters." Seven items followed, the first of which read, "How the saboteurs were so swiftly apprehended."[37] The Biddle-Cramer statement further notes, "We do not propose to tell our enemies the answers to the questions which are puzzling them." Certainly one of the puzzles in the minds of Nazi authorities was how the American government could round up the eight men so quickly. To top officials, the reason was obvious: Dasch had turned himself (and the others) in. Biddle did not want that information made public.

Davis, disappointed with the restrictions on the press, asked for a meeting with Roosevelt. On July 9, the President met with Stimson, Davis, and Steve Early (Roosevelt's press secretary), proposing that

33. Id. at 145.
34. Id.
35. "Rules Established by the Military Commission Appointed by Order of the President of July 2, 1942," at 1, Papers of Frank Ross McCoy, Box 79, LC (hereafter McCoy Papers).
36. July 8, 1942, Statement, Court Room, Department of Justice, McCoy Papers.
37. Untitled, undated three-page statement, at 3, McCoy Papers. The same language appears in "Proposed Statement for Elmer Davis," id.

the tribunal issue brief communiqués but eliminate any factual evidence that might be dangerous to national security. Davis reopened the issue of three witnesses from the press, but Roosevelt turned him down.[38]

Each day the tribunal issued a terse communiqué about what had happened in the morning and the afternoon. One other slight exception to the rule of secrecy was allowed. On July 11, the tribunal allowed eleven reporters to enter Room 5235 for fifteen minutes to snap photographs, take notes, and get a sense of who sat where. Brig. Gen. Albert L. Cox, provost marshal of the Military District of Washington, D.C., pointed to the prisoners and identified them. What impressed many observers about the eight men was their ordinariness. When Lewis Wood of the *New York Times* entered the courtroom with the other reporters, he thought that he might see "a burly, booted Storm Trooper, a brutal U-boat captain," or someone resembling the "ruthless, blond German glorified by Hitler." Instead, he gazed upon "merely a group of most ordinary-looking individuals." Haupt, he said, looked "like any petty defendant in a police court."[39] Royall, toward the end of the trial, said this about Heinck: "he is just one of those people who fell into the stream and could not do much but follow it. We have them everywhere. We run into them in the army."[40] The reporters had an opportunity to ask Cox a few questions and to examine the evidence piled on a table.[41] Then it was back to business.

Although the trial was held in secret, one part of the proceedings became highly visible: transporting the prisoners back and forth from the D.C. jail to the Justice Department. The eight men traveled in two covered black vans following a carload of FBI agents, an Army scout car (with soldiers holding tommy guns), and two mounted machine guns directed at the vans. On the rear platform of

38. Stimson Diary, July 9, 1942, at 152–53.
39. "Spy Court Session Viewed by Press," New York Times, July 12, 1942, at 1.
40. Military Trial, at 2817.
41. "Spy Court Session Viewed by Press," New York Times, July 12, 1942, at 1; "Spies Fidget as Reporters Visit Military Courtroom," Washington Post, July 12, 1942, at 1.

each van stood an armed solder. Nine motorcycle policemen provided an escort. Regardless of the different routes taken, crowds
formed to watch the procession, with vendors along the side of the
road selling their merchandise. The vans entered the driveway leading to the courtyard of the Justice Department.

Setting Some Ground Rules

By the time the trial began, the defense team of Dowell and Royall
had been augmented with two other officers: Maj. Lauson H. Stone
(son of Chief Justice Stone) and Capt. William G. Hummell. This
foursome defended only seven of the Germans. Dasch, by cooperating with the government, gained his own attorney: Colonel Ristine.
One might have expected the two defense teams to cooperate with
each other and present a united front against the prosecutors. However, frequently the strategy of one defense team interfered with and
jeopardized the work of the other. In addition to raising objections
to steps taken by the prosecution, the two defense teams objected to
efforts by each other.

Even before the commission could swear itself in, Royall took
the floor to state his belief that Roosevelt's order creating the commission "is invalid and unconstitutional." Drawing on the principles
established by the Supreme Court in *Ex parte Milligan,* he stated
that the civil courts in the District of Columbia were open and questioned the jurisdiction of any court except a civil court. Moreover,
he charged that Roosevelt's order "violates in several specific particulars congressional enactments as reflected in the Articles of
War."[42]

Biddle, taken aback by Royall's quick initiative, said that he
could not conceive that a military commission "composed of high
officers of the Army, under a commission signed by the
Commander-in-Chief, would listen to argument on the question of
its power under that authority to try these defendants." Bottom line:

42. Military Trial, at 5.

generals obey the President. Biddle then stumbled on the role to be played by civil courts. He first said that "the question of law involved is a question, of course, to be determined by the civil courts should it be presented to the civil courts." Having implied that some questions might be addressed by civil courts, he tried to slam the door shut: "this is not a trial of offenses of law of the civil courts but is a trial of the offenses of the law of war, which is not cognizable to the civil courts."[43]

Royall hit a touchy—if not raw—point by questioning the competence of the members of the commission to try a case when they served directly under the President as Commander in Chief. Royall posed the point delicately by asking whether any member had "to any degree the feeling that the circumstances under which the Commission is appointed would make it difficult or embarrassing for him to reach a judgment in favor of the defendants in the event the evidence should so indicate."[44] The commission members answered no. Royall proceeded to ask whether "the fact that this trial is being conducted in time of war would in any manner incline the commission to deal more harshly with the defendants in the matter of conviction or sentence than they would if it were in time of peace." After General McCoy ruled that this was not a proper question, Royall said that he had "no challenge for cause."[45]

Attorneys customarily challenge jurors for cause and also make "peremptory strikes" that can eliminate potential jurors without stating a reason. After Royall found no challenge for cause, his co-counsel Dowell stood up and asked for one peremptory challenge, as allowed under the 18th Article of War for a court-martial. Biddle countered that it was up to the commission to decide whether to grant or refuse any peremptory challenges. Cramer agreed that the defense had no right to a peremptory challenge but said that he had no objection "as a matter of procedure." McCoy ruled that the commission would not entertain a peremptory challenge from either side.[46]

43. Id.
44. Id. at 14.
45. Id.
46. Id. at 14–18.

Why this issue of peremptory challenges came up on July 8 is curious. The tribunal had adopted some sketchy rules the previous day, including this provision: "(a) No peremptory challenge shall be allowed. (b) Challenge of members of the Commission for cause may be permitted. The Commission, by a two-thirds vote of those voting—the challenged member not voting—may pass on any challenge."[47] Was Dowell unaware of this rule, or did he simply want to go on record to challenge the tribunal and thus lay the groundwork for an appeal to civil court?

McCoy continued to issue rulings in response to various questions raised by the two sides, often against the defendants but at times against the prosecution. The general message became quite clear. The commission could jettison procedures from the Articles of War and the *Manual for Courts-Martial* whenever it wanted to. As Cramer told the commission at one point, "Of course, if the Commission please, the Commission has discretion to do anything it pleases; there is no dispute about that."[48]

After the commission was sworn in, it proceeded to swear in the counsels. Biddle and Cramer were asked whether they would faithfully and impartially perform their duties and "not divulge the findings or sentence of this Military Commission to any but the proper authority until they shall be duly disclosed."[49] The words "proper authority" allowed them to talk to President Roosevelt and other high officials. Royall had some misgivings about the oath put to him. He told the commission that "it is possible that some limited disclosure would have to be made if someone sought to assert the civil rights of these defendants; and we conceive it our duty not to take an oath that would prevent us from so doing."[50] He had in mind the possibility not only that he would personally go to the civil court but also that he might have to designate someone from the private sector to do that. Royall asked for and received the same language used for Biddle

47. "Rules Established by the Military Commission Appointed by Order of the President of July 2, 1942, at 3, McCoy Papers.
48. Military Trial, at 991.
49. Id. at 19.
50. Id. at 20.

and Cramer.[51] In his case, "the proper authority" might cover a district judge or the Justices of the Supreme Court. The prospect of Royall going to district court to challenge the constitutionality of Roosevelt's proclamation hung in the air throughout the trial.

Articles of War/Law of War

The government charged the eight Germans with four crimes: one against the "law of war," two against the Articles of War (81st and 82nd), and one involving conspiracy. The prosecutors thus combined a mix of offenses that were nonstatutory (law of war) and statutory (Articles of War). The distinction here is fundamental. In federal law, the creation of criminal offenses is reserved to the legislative branch, not to the President. The Constitution vests in Congress the power to "define and punish Piracies and Felonies committed on the high Seas, and Offences on Land and Water."[52] By enacting the Articles of War, Congress defined not only the procedures but also the punishments for the field of military law. Charging individuals with violations of the "law of war" shifts the balance of power from Congress to the Executive.

In enacting Articles of War, Congress depended on British precedents dating back to the 1650s. Parliament amended those Articles in 1749 and again in 1757. The purpose of the Articles was to set down penalties for various acts by soldiers and sailors and to establish procedures for courts-martial. Punishments were meted out for failure to obey orders, mutinous practices, and other conduct that required discipline.[53] When George Washington served as an officer in the American colonies under British rule, it was his duty to have these Articles of War read to recruits.[54] He was also responsible for

51. Id. at 20–21.
52. U.S. Const., art. I, § 8, cl. 10.
53. 19 Statutes at Large 325–39 (Cambridge, England: 1765); 22 Statutes at Large 227–34 (Cambridge, England: 1766).
54. Orders of December 25, 1755, in Writings of George Washington 1:257, ed. John C. Fitzpatrick (Washington, D.C.: Government Printing Office, 1931).

supervising general courts-martial and approving the sentences that were handed down.[55]

In 1775, with the American colonies preparing to declare independence from England, the Continental Congress adopted rules and regulations for the military, drawing these principles of warfare from the British Articles of War.[56] Legislative control over the Articles of War is evident in the action of the Continental Congress on April 14, 1777, when it decided that no sentence of a general court-martial could be executed until a report was first made to Congress, the Commander in Chief, or the continental general commanding in the state.[57] George Washington, as the Commander in Chief, followed the Articles of War enacted by the Continental Congress and reviewed sentences issued by courts-martial.[58]

After ratification of the U.S. Constitution, one of the first actions of the new Congress was to pass legislation in 1789 stating that military troops "shall be governed by the rules and articles of war which have been established by the United States in Congress assembled, or by such rules and articles of war, as may hereafter by law be established."[59] In 1806, in the exercise of this legislative authority, Congress established "Rules and Articles for the Government of the Armies of the United States." The statute consisted of 101 articles. For example, under Article 87, no person "shall be sentenced to suffer death, but by the concurrence of two-thirds of the members of a general court-martial."[60] At the time of the Nazi saboteur case, the penalty of death required a unanimous vote of a court-martial. In another provision of interest for the saboteur case, the 1806 statute provided that in time of war, "all persons not citizens of, or owing allegiance to the United States of America, who shall be found lurking as spies, in or about the fortifications or encampments of the armies of the United States, or any of them, shall

55. Id. at 354 (Orders of May 2, 1756).
56. Journals of the Continental Congress 2:111–23 (Washington, D.C.: Government Printing Office, 1905).
57. Id. at 7:265.
58. Writings of George Washington, at 13:136–40.
59. 1 Stat. 96, § 4 (1789).
60. 2 Stat. 368, Art. 87 (1806).

suffer death, according to the law and usage of nations, by sentence of death."[61] Much of this language is reflected in the charges against the Nazi saboteurs.

The text of the four charges against the Nazi saboteurs, reproduced below, underscores the legal importance of the Germans using civilian dress and fake names. Charge I ("Violation of the Law of War") consists of two specifications, drawing from general principles of international law. It reads as follows:

Specification 1. In that, during the month of June 1942, Edward John Kerling (and others) being enemies of the United States and acting for and on behalf of the German Reich, a belligerent enemy nation, secretly and covertly passed, in civilian dress, contrary to the law of war, through the military and naval lines and defenses of the United States, along the Atlantic Coast, and went behind such lines and defenses in civilian dress within zones of military operations and elsewhere, for the purpose of committing acts of sabotage, espionage, and other hostile acts, and, in particular, to destroy certain war industries, war utilities, and war materials within the United States.

Specification 2. In that, during the month of June 1942, Edward John Kerling (and others), being enemies of the United States and acting for and on behalf of the German Reich, a belligerent enemy nation, appeared, contrary to the law of war, behind the military and naval defenses and lines of the United States, within the zones of military operations and elsewhere, for the purpose of committing or attempting to commit sabotage, espionage, and other hostile acts, without being in the uniform of the armed forces of the German Reich, and planned and attempted to destroy and sabotage war industries, war utilities, and war materials within the United States, and assembled together within the United States explosives, money, and other supplies in order to accomplish said purposes.

Specification 2 tracks much of Specification 1 but speaks more broadly of not merely "committing" acts but "committing or *attempting* to commit" them. It also mentions the availability of explosives, money, and other supplies to accomplish those objectives.

The next two charges draw from the Articles of War enacted by Congress. Charge II ("Violation of the 81st Article of War") goes

61. Id. at 372, Art. 101 (2).

beyond sabotage efforts to the communicating of intelligence with one another and to enemies of the United States. The verb "relieve" in this charge is used in the legal sense of "to assist."

Specification: In that, during the month of June 1942, Edward John Kerling (and others), being enemies of the United States and acting for and on behalf of the German Reich, a belligerent enemy nation, and without being in the uniform of the armed forces of that nation, relieved or attempted to relieve enemies of the United States with arms, ammunition, supplies, money and other things, and knowingly harbored, protected and held correspondence with and gave intelligence to enemies of the United States by entering the territorial limits of the United States, in the company of other enemies of the United States, with explosives, money, and other supplies with which they relieved each other and relieved the German Reich, for the purpose of destroying and sabotaging war industries, transportation facilities, or war materials of the United States, and by harboring, communicating with, and giving intelligence to each other and to other enemies of the United States in the course of such activities.

Charge III ("Violation of the 82nd Article of War") focuses on spying and attempting to communicate information to Nazi Germany:

Specification: In that, during the month of June 1942, Edward John Kerling (and others), being enemies of the United States and acting for and on behalf of the German Reich, a belligerent enemy nation, were, in time of war, found lurking or acting as spies in or about the fortifications, posts, and encampments of the armies of the United States and elsewhere, and secretly and covertly passed through the military and naval lines and defenses of the United States, along the Atlantic Coast, and went about, through, and behind said lines and defenses and about the fortifications, posts, and encampments of the armies of the United States, in zones of military operations and elsewhere, disguised in civilian clothes and under false names, for the purpose of committing sabotage and other hostile acts against the United States, and for the purpose of communicating intelligence relating to such sabotage and other hostile acts to each other, to the German Reich, and to other enemies of the United States, during the course of such activities and thereafter.

Charge IV ("Conspiracy to Commit All of the Above Acts") states:

Specification: In that, during the year 1942, Edward John Kerling (and others), being enemies of the United States and acting for and on behalf of the German Reich, a belligerent enemy nation, did plot, plan, and conspire with each other, with the German Reich, and with other enemies of the United States, to commit each and every one of the above-enumerated charges and specifications.

Charges I and III claimed that the eight Germans were "within zones of military operations," behind the military and naval defense lines of the United States, or "about the fortifications, posts, and encampments" of U.S. military forces. Royall and Ristine denied that the men had been in those locations. As to encountering the Coast Guardsman at Amagansett, Royall argued that because Cullen had not been armed, the patrol was not a zone of military operation.[62]

Progress in the trial stalled at one point when Ristine learned that the prosecutors had introduced two of Dasch's statements in the record but withheld a third. Not wanting the government to pick and choose among the statements to be entered, Ristine insisted that this third statement be introduced. Biddle strongly objected, pointing out that this statement should be withheld from the record because it was too long (254 single-spaced pages), largely irrelevant, and "self-serving."[63] The tribunal, which had been ruling fairly consistently against motions offered by the defendants, agreed to accommodate Ristine's request. The statement was introduced in connection with the cross-examination.[64] Ristine then surprised the tribunal by saying that Dasch wanted the statement *read* "in its entirety" into the record.[65] None of the other statements had been read into the record, and Biddle protested again, but the tribunal—perhaps only vaguely aware of the magnitude of the undertaking—again deferred to Ristine.[66]

Over the course of one afternoon, the entire next day, and the morning of the third, the bloated Dasch statement was read into the

62. Military Trial, at 119.
63. Id. at 604.
64. Id. at 1003.
65. Id. at 1016, 1019.
66. Id. at 1023.

record. Ristine could not be expected to do all the reading, so several others pitched in, including members of the prosecution team. At several points, the trial transcript notes that Biddle refused to be in the room during this reading, a decision that must have annoyed the members of the tribunal, who had to sit through every moment of this excruciating, mind-numbing ordeal. Press stories commented on this phase of the trial. The *New York Times* reported that the "morning session was devoted largely to finishing the reading of a long statement begun Wednesday."[67] The *Washington Post* said this about one of the confessions: "One of these was so long in its fantastic detail that it took almost two days to read."[68]

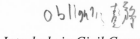

Interlude in Civil Court

Royall had several times indicated to the tribunal that he might go to civil court to test the constitutionality of Roosevelt's proclamation and order. On the afternoon of Tuesday, July 21, after the defendants had been removed from the courtroom, Royall told the military commission what he planned to do. From the *Manual for Courts-Martial,* he read that an officer acting as counsel for the accused had an obligation to perform "such duties as usually devolve upon the counsel for a defendant before civil courts in a criminal case." It was incumbent upon the counsel to guard the accused's interests "by all honorable and legitimate means known to the law."[69] Did this mean that Royall had an obligation to take the case to civil court?

Royall had wrestled with that issue before the trial began. On July 6, he and Dowell wrote to President Roosevelt that "there is a serious legal doubt as to the constitutionality and validity of the Proclamation and as to the constitutionality and validity of the Order." It was their opinion that the defendants "should have an opportunity to institute an appropriate proceeding to test the constitutionality and

67. "Long Island Phase of Spy Trial Ends," New York Times, July 18, 1942, at 7.
68. "U.S. Rests Its Case Against 4 at Spy Trial," Washington Post, July 18, 1942, at 1.
69. Military Trial, at 2099.

re.lues, i7♮ Ⅱ

validity of the Proclamation and of the Order." Could Royall and Dowell, as military officers, act in a manner contrary to the wishes of the Commander in Chief? They told Roosevelt, "In view of the fact that our appointment is made on the same Order which appoints the Military Commission, the question arises as to whether we are authorized to institute the proceeding suggested above." Requesting that he issue to them or to someone else the appropriate authority, they closed by noting that they had advised Biddle, Cramer, the commission, and Stimson of their intention to present the matter to the President.[70] They also requested a meeting with Roosevelt, but he refused.[71]

In response to their letter, Biddle advised Roosevelt that it would be a "mistake" to deny them authority to seek redress in civil courts, for it "might tend to give the public impression that the prisoners are not being given a fair trial." Second, if Roosevelt denied them access, it would imply that the proclamation of July 2 was "not clear, and, therefore, would in substance amend your original order" (giving Biddle and Stimson discretion to grant access to civil courts).[72] Biddle next advised Roosevelt to tell Royall and Dowell that the proclamation and order were clear and "that the problem of interpretation—if any—is one within their province as defense counsel." Biddle added that if he were representing the eight Germans, he would have "no hesitation in construing the Order to permit me to petition for habeas corpus if I thought it wise to do so." If Royall and Dowell doubted that course of action, Biddle said, Roosevelt could advise them to use "their own best judgment as to whether they should try to petition for habeas corpus, just as counsel can in any case."[73] Biddle drafted a letter with that language.[74]

70. Letter of July 6, 1942, Military Trial, at 2099.

71. Stimson Diary, July 6, 1942, at 144.

72. Letter of July 6, 1942, from Biddle to Roosevelt, at 1, "German Saboteur" file, RG 107, Office of the Secretary of War, Stimson "Safe File," National Archives, College Park, Md.

73. Id. at 2.

74. Suggested memorandum for the President's signature, Memorandum to Colonel Cassius M. Dowell and Colonel Kenneth C. Royall, Stimson "Safe File."

Instead of responding by letter, Roosevelt asked one of his aides, Marvin McIntyre, to call Royall and Dowell and advise them to act in accordance with their own judgment. They incorporated that understanding in a letter written to Roosevelt on July 7, stating that it was their conclusion that they had the necessary authority and also the duty to "try to arrange for civil counsel to institute the proceedings necessary to determine the constitutionality and validity of the Proclamation and Order of July 2." If those arrangements could not be made, they said that they would institute those proceedings "ourselves at the appropriate time." Unless ordered otherwise by Roosevelt, "we will act accordingly."[75] They heard nothing more from Roosevelt.

By the time the trial reached its twelfth day, Royall decided to bring the matter to a head. He first advised the tribunal that he had been unable to secure civilian counsel. Second, he announced that he had prepared papers for an application for a writ of habeas corpus to test the constitutionality and validity of the proclamation and order. He drafted the papers to reveal "nothing more about the proceedings here than is absolutely necessary for the assertion of the rights which we think ought to be asserted."[76] With regard to secrecy concerns, he expressed a willingness to show the draft petition to the commission but not to the Attorney General.

Dowell stood up to explain that he could not support Royall's decision. He told the tribunal that he had been a soldier for over forty years and was accustomed to taking orders from the Commander in Chief. He thought Royall's petition was "honorable and correct, but not legitimate, as far as I am concerned." It was Dowell's judgment that the proclamation closed the doors of civil courts to the defendants. He recognized that the proclamation made an exception at the end, to be made by the recommendation of the Attorney General with the approval of the Secretary of War. Without their support, there seemed to be no hope for a test case in the civilian courts. Moreover, Dowell expressed concern that any

75. Letter of July 7, 1942, Military Trial, at 2102.
76. Military Trial, at 2104.

publicity created by taking the matter to a civilian court "will injure our national cause, our war effort. As a soldier I cannot bring myself to the point of doing that."[77] Despite those statements, Dowell worked with Royall on the appeal to the Supreme Court.

Ristine also broke with Royall on the appeal to civilian courts. Although he was there to represent Dasch, he stated, "I do not construe those orders as authorizing me to file in any other tribunal any application for a writ of habeas corpus or other proceeding, and therefore I stand on that interpretation of my orders."[78] Ristine, coming late to the case, thought that any effort to pursue a petition for a writ of habeas corpus would be done by outside counsel or civilian lawyers.

Royall, seemingly standing alone, told the tribunal that he was going to do what he had outlined in the memo to Roosevelt unless someone ordered him not to do it, "because that is what I conceive my duty to be."[79] He further explained that he was not asking for the advice of the tribunal and was not asking it to remove any oath of secrecy. He was merely asking the tribunal to examine the proposed petition to see if it improperly disclosed any facts. If the tribunal chose not to examine it, that was fine with Royall. He would proceed as he had announced. With the petition sitting on the table, the commission members closed the proceedings and discussed the matter among themselves. Upon their return, they told Royall, "The commission does not care to pass on that question."[80]

As time began to run out, Royall started contacting Justices of the Supreme Court to see if they were willing to meet in special session in the middle of the summer to take up the question. He first met with Hugo Black at the Justice's home in Alexandria, Virginia, receiving some encouragement. The next step was a meeting on July 23 with Black at Justice Roberts's farm outside Philadelphia. Dowell, Biddle, and Cramer joined them.[81] To accommodate their

77. Id. at 2108–10.
78. Id. at 2110.
79. Id. at 2111.
80. Id. at 2114.
81. David J. Danelski, "The Saboteurs' Case," 1 Journal of Supreme Court History 61, 68 (1996).

trip, the tribunal did not sit on July 23. After Roberts and Black discussed the matter with Biddle and Royall, Roberts phoned Chief Justice Harlan Fiske Stone and reached a decision: the Court would hear oral argument on Wednesday, July 29.[82]

All this had been agreed to without any action by a lower federal court. Royall seemed to think that he could present the dispute to Justice Black, sitting on circuit, and go directly from there to the Supreme Court. Justice Roberts sent Royall a phone message with a citation to *Marbury* v. *Madison,* flagging what should have been obvious: the Court lacked direct jurisdiction over the case.[83] At that point, Royall put the issue in front of a federal district court in the District of Columbia, asking permission to file a petition for a writ of habeas corpus for the seven defendants he represented. On July 28, at 8 p.m., District Judge James W. Morris issued a brief statement denying permission, stating that the defendants came within a category—subjects, citizens, or residents of a nation at war with the United States—that, under Roosevelt's proclamation, is "not privileged to seek any remedy or maintain any proceeding in the courts of the United States." The judge did not consider *Ex parte Milligan* "controlling in the circumstances of this petitioner."[84]

With the heads-up at Justice Roberts's farm, the Supreme Court made plans to hold oral argument, which began at noon on July 29. The details of the nine hours of oral argument are covered in the next chapter, which looks at every phase of the Court's work: briefs prepared by the parties, oral argument on July 29 and 30, the per curiam decision on July 31 that upheld the jurisdiction of the military tribunal, and the long, drawn-out effort to write a decision explaining the legal basis for the July 31 per curiam. That decision would not appear until October 29.

But the tribunal had what it needed to complete the trial. The July 31 per curiam stated that the Court had "fully considered" the questions raised and "now announces its decision and enters its

82. Id.

83. Alpheus Thomas Mason, "Inter Arma Silent Leges: Chief Justice Stone's Views," 69 Harvard Law Review 806, 818 n. 49 (1956).

84. Ex parte Quirin, 47 F.Supp. 431 (D.D.C. 1942).

judgment in each case, in advance of the preparation of a full opinion which necessarily will require a considerable period of time for its preparation." The ruling upheld President Roosevelt's authority to create the commission and denied the motions for leave to file petitions for writs of habeas corpus.[85]

Windup of the Trial

During the remaining days of the trial, each defendant took the stand and testified that he had no plans to conduct sabotage in the United States. Some conceded that they had intended to commit sabotage during training in Germany but had changed their minds on the submarine coming over or after reaching America. A few, such as Dasch and Burger, claimed that they had joined the sabotage team to get out of Germany and find safety in the United States. Burger, because of his treatment by the Gestapo, could offer that explanation with some credibility. When Royall asked him whether it was his intent to get out of Germany, Burger answered, "Get out and get even."[86] Heinck told the tribunal that he wanted to return to America because he "liked the liberty of this country, the freedom over here, what we did not have in Germany."[87] These statements could not overcome the fact that all eight had enjoyed freedom in the United States and chose to return to the Fatherland, often willing to endure arduous and dangerous journeys by traveling to Japan, through Russia, and on to Berlin.

Two of the defendants, Thiel and Kerling, testified that FBI agent Donegan had "mistreated" them with slaps and hair-pulling.[88] Kerling said that he had signed the confession because he was too weak to read it carefully.[89] Donegan took the stand to deny that he

85. Ex parte Quirin, 63 S.Ct. 1–2 (1942). The per curiam is also reproduced in a footnote in Ex parte Quirin, 317 U.S. 1, 18–19 (1942).
86. Military Trial, at 2683.
87. Id. at 2457.
88. Id. at 2265–68, 2304, 2333–37.
89. Id. at 2338.

had pulled a defendant's hair or slapped him. He admitted to talking "rough."[90] These claims by the defendants were not very convincing. The accusations seemed to be a strained, last-ditch effort by defense counsel to discredit the charges put forth by the prosecution and place a shadow over the confessions.

In the closing days of the trial, Royall made additional efforts to challenge the validity of the charges. He introduced into evidence a confidential letter from the Adjutant General, stating that the Eastern Theatre of Operations had been changed to the Eastern Defense Command, which "will not be a Theatre of Operations." Royall used this letter to argue that the eight men had not conducted themselves as spies because they had not been in a theatre of operations.[91] Biddle and Cramer countered with other exhibits and brought in a witness, Col. Stephen H. Sherrill, to explain that the change in designation had to do with supplies and that, in a tactical sense, the Eastern Defense Command was still a theatre of operations.[92] His testimony was sufficiently dense, technical, and bureaucratic to neutralize Royall's claim.

These arguments were offered through Monday, July 27. The tribunal did not meet on Tuesday, Wednesday, and Thursday because of the appeals to the district court and the two days of oral argument before the Supreme Court. The trial resumed on Friday morning, July 31, with the Court scheduled to hand down its decision. In his opening argument, Cramer stated that the evidence supported a finding of guilt and a sentence of death in each case. The men had come through the Atlantic Ocean, "which we all know at the present time is a theatre of operations at sea, where ships are being sunk." When they reached American shores, had the defense force been stronger, it could have attacked the submarines, "and they could have been attacked and shot down as an invading force."[93]

90. Id. at 2759.
91. Id. at 2708.
92. Id. at 2746–51.
93. Id. at 2767–68.

Royall and Dowell. As Royall began his argument, he discussed the difficulty of defending seven men—all with different circumstances—so that "what is said in favor of one may not be favorable to another or may be positively unfavorable." He said that he should not have been in a position "of arraying one of our clients against the other," yet Burger's case seemed to him "to stand alone and requires separate and different consideration." To some extent, he thought that was also true of Haupt.[94] Although the Supreme Court had not yet released its decision, Royall underscored that no other court except the tribunal "can possibly determine the facts, the weight to be given the testimony." None of the parties before the Supreme Court expected it to "pass upon the weight of the evidence or the facts to be found from the evidence."[95] The writ of habeas corpus raised only the question of jurisdiction, not issues of facts and evidence.

Royall reminded the tribunal that the *Manual for Courts-Martial* provided that in order to convict someone of an offense, the court must be satisfied of guilt beyond a reasonable doubt. Nothing in Roosevelt's order, he said, altered that standard "in any degree."[96] He did not think that the charge of spying had been proved. He also cautioned the tribunal to act in a manner that would protect Americans brought up before foreign tribunals. The United States was moving into the zone of military operations on other continents, "and the chances are that American soldiers will have to face this situation much more frequently than will the enemy agents." The tribunal's decision "may establish a criterion which will be applicable, ten to one, to our own boys who are going overseas."[97]

To Royall, the eight men did nothing to deserve the death penalty. "They did not hurt anybody. They did not blow up anything."[98] He reviewed the legal distinction between what someone intends to

94. Id. at 2770.
95. Id. at 2772.
96. Id. at 2774.
97. Id. at 2775–77.
98. Id. at 2777–78.

do and what he actually does. Whoever shoots and kills someone can be put to death. If the person shoots and misses, he will get a few years. If a person buys a pistol with the intent to kill, he might be fined $50. Many people, he said, have wished someone dead, but the act of carrying out murder requires "much more hardness, much more criminality, much more depravity."[99] He said that there was considerable doubt whether any of the eight men had the criminality or depravity to carry out sabotage. "Let us not let the fact of war absolutely change the character of what they have done. Give it weight, yes; but do not let it destroy our entire perspective of just exactly what has happened."[100]

Royall pointed out that Congress had enacted a statute on sabotage "with the war fully in view." It proposed a maximum penalty in time of peace and a maximum penalty in time of war. The maximum for the latter was thirty years. "These men have not done anywhere near that much."[101] They had not attempted to commit sabotage, "because an attempt is distinguished from preparation." Buying a gun to kill someone is not an attempt, he said. It violates the law, but it "is not an attempt to commit murder."[102] Although Royall agreed that the statute did not bind the tribunal, he called it a legitimate and fair guide for the tribunal's deliberation and decision. Because the United States was fighting World War II "to preserve our own system of government," it was important to administer procedures "with equity and justice in times of stress as well as in times of peace and quiet." He urged the tribunal not to be a "fair-weather government."[103] The United States, he predicted, would win the war, but it should not "want to win it by throwing away everything we are fighting for, because we will have a mighty empty victory if we destroy the genuineness and the truth of democratic government and fair administration of law." The real test of a system of justice "is not when the sun is shining but is when the

99. Id. at 2779.
100. Id. at 2781.
101. Id. at 2782–83.
102. Id. at 2783.
103. Id. at 2784–85.

weather is stormy."[104] Royall told the tribunal that anything he said about spying in a zone of operations would be secondhand information that Dowell had given him, so he turned that part of the argument over to his partner.

Regarding Charge III about spying, Dowell insisted that the tribunal was bound by the regulation that explained Article of War 82. Certain elements of spying had to be satisfied. The accused must be found at a certain place within a zone of operations and must act clandestinely, or under false pretenses. He must obtain, or endeavor to obtain, information with intent to communicate the information to the enemy. The act of "obtaining" was not satisfied by getting ready to obtain, and "endeavoring to obtain" meant a serious attempt.[105] None of those specifications appeared in Charge III. He quoted also from the *Manual for Courts-Martial:* "Soliciting another to commit a crime is not an attempt; nor is mere preparation to do a criminal act." As an analogy, he said that someone buying matches to set a haystack on fire was not making an attempt. It was preparation.[106]

Dowell identified other elements of spying that were not present with regard to the eight men. The information sought must be of a military nature, and it must be material information. "If it is immaterial, it would not constitute the act of spying at all."[107] If the spying did not occur in a theatre of operations, "the offense of spying is not triable by this tribunal." He quoted this language from an opinion by Attorney General T. W. Gregory in 1918: "in this country, military tribunals, whether courts-martial or military commissions, can not constitutionally be granted jurisdiction to try persons charged with acts of offences committed outside of the field of military operations."[108]

To minimize the damage done by Gregory's language, the Justice Department on July 29, 1942, released a previously unpublished

104. Id. at 2785.
105. Id. at 2791.
106. Id. at 2792.
107. Id.
108. Id. at 2796; 31 Ops. Att'y Gen. 356 (1918).

Attorney General opinion, dated December 24, 1919, taking the op-
posite position.[109] What Dowell and Royall had relied on (a published Attorney General opinion) was now useless. A few days after
releasing the 1919 opinion, Oscar Cox drafted a memo for Biddle,
giving further details on why the Justice Department decided to re-
pudiate Gregory's opinion and to do so without public admission.[110]

Royall reinforced Dowell's points by distinguishing between
spying and espionage. Although popular dictionaries treated them
as identical, congressional statutes did not. Spying had to be committed in a zone of military operations and had to involve information of a direct military nature, such as the number of troops sent
into combat. Espionage covered other activities, such as giving information to the enemy about the manufacturing capacity of a plant
that produces munitions. Six of the Germans had no ability to communicate with the enemy. Only the two group leaders, Dasch and
Kerling, had been given the handkerchiefs with the secret writing
identifying the contact in Lisbon. It could be argued that Burger,
had he placed ads in the newspaper as planned, could have been in
touch with Kappe. There had been discussion at the Quenz farm of
giving the men radio instruction, but that part of the program had
been canceled.[111]

After a recess from 11:40 a.m. to 1:30 p.m., Royall announced
that the Supreme Court had held that the commission possessed jurisdiction to try the eight men. He then focused on Charge II, involving Article of War 81: assisting the enemy with arms, ammunition, supplies, money, "and other things," or knowingly harboring
or protecting or holding correspondence with or giving intelligence
to the enemy. Royall said that the statute was constitutional only if
confined to the area of military jurisdiction. There was no evidence
that the men had given money to the enemy and no evidence that
they had given any intelligence to the enemy or communicated with
the enemy. The buried explosives did not assist the enemy because

109. 40 Ops. Att'y Gen. 561 (1919), released for publication July 29, 1942.
110. Memo from Cox to Biddle, July 2, 1942, and from Biddle to Alexander Holt-
zoff, July 2, 1942, Papers of Oscar Cox, Box 61, FDR Library.
111. Military Trial, at 2801–5.

they were not immediately usable, Royall said. They had to be assembled and moved somewhere.[112] Regarding Charge I on violating the "law of war," Royall objected that he had not been given the opportunity of knowing "just what law of war is charged to have been violated."[113]

Ristine. As for Dasch's guilt, Ristine said that when Dasch left some secret matches (used for invisible writing) on a table in the submarine, he "absolutely deprived himself, if he had ever had any intention of writing back to Kappe, of the only means by which they had agreed upon for communication."[114] Dasch, he said, had not paid attention to instructions at the school and could not have implemented the sabotage plan. Also, to stay in touch with Kappe, he had to give the name of someone in the United States that Kerling could reach if he lost touch with Dasch. At Kappe's suggestion, Dasch had given his brother's address, but a fictitious one.

The prosecution argued that if Dasch had contacted the FBI immediately upon arriving, the government might have intercepted the submarine in Florida. Said Ristine: "Let us see. The Florida coast, as I recall it, is between 500 and 700 miles long, along the Atlantic Ocean. Just how anybody is going down there and apprehend a submarine that is going to discharge a few passengers some night on a coast that big, I do not know."[115]

Final Day. The trial now moved to its last day: Saturday, August 1. In his summation, Royall again singled out Burger from the other defendants he represented. Although he claimed that Burger was not guilty of the charges, he recommended that Burger be interned as an alien enemy.[116] As to the other six, he said that they were not guilty, and "none of them is guilty of an offense which requires the most severe punishment." He thought that Haupt's age "in itself

112. Id. at 2808–11.
113. Id. at 2809.
114. Id. at 2827.
115. Id. at 2875–76.
116. Id. at 2923.

would justify a distinction, whose American citizenship would in itself justify a distinction." If Haupt was not acquitted, "he ought to receive a very minor punishment."[117]

In the closing argument for the prosecution, Cramer emphasized the need to punish the men as a preventive measure. They had described their effort as "the first of a series of these schools; that others were coming over here later."[118] As for the thirty-year maximum punishment for sabotage, Cramer said that the statute was not exclusive. The commission could consider a heavier punishment under the law of war. Turning to Haupt's claim that he had come back to the United States because he wanted to be here, Cramer noted that the first thing he had done "was to take some pills to do something to evade the draft."[119] Cramer also challenged Royall's description of the limited competence of the eight men: "I cannot conceive it possible that a man with Kappe's ability and the position he had would seek to take an outfit of this kind and send it abroad—an expedition of this kind, constituting simply eight morons, as you might say, who had no intention of going through with this at all."[120] As for Dasch, his change of heart might have come from the encounter with the Coast Guardsman, convincing him that "they were going to be caught."[121] Had Dasch contacted the FBI right away, the Florida coast would have been "more closely watched, with a much better possibility of apprehending" the second submarine.[122]

The defendants testified that they had agreed to join the saboteur school because a refusal would have placed family and friends in jeopardy. Cramer dismissed that story: "How much are they going to protect their families by having come over like this and [been] turned in to the United States than if they had gone out illegally, as they call it? Their families are going to be in the same position, if

117. Id. at 2926.
118. Id. at 2930.
119. Id. at 2947.
120. Id. at 2949.
121. Id. at 2950.
122. Id. at 2951.

not worse, because of the fact that they discarded the plan when they got over here."[123] He recommended the death penalty for all eight. The talk about a presidential pardon for Dasch, he said, was "immaterial." The commission was merely being asked whether the men were guilty of the offenses charged. As to the assistance that some of them may have given to the FBI, that raised "a matter of clemency" for the President to decide.[124] Biddle argued that espionage did not require the defendants to actually obtain information or communicate it. It was enough, he said, that they communicated among themselves.[125] He concurred with Cramer in asking for the death penalty. The commission closed the trial at 2:25 p.m.

Sentencing and Execution

After the military trial concluded on August 1, the members of the tribunal began their deliberations. Two days later, after deciding that all eight men were guilty and deserved the death penalty, they submitted their verdict to Roosevelt, along with 3,000 pages of trial proceedings. Roosevelt looked through the material on August 4, with the assistance of Samuel Rosenman and other aides.[126] Joining in those discussions were J. Edgar Hoover, James H. Rowe, Jr., Oscar Cox, Frank Ross McCoy, and Myron C. Cramer.[127] Conversing with aide William Hassett, Roosevelt wondered about the appropriate method of execution for the saboteurs: "Should they be shot or hanged?" Hassett recommended hanging because shooting was "too honorable a death." Roosevelt raised another issue: "What about pictures?" Hassett wanted pictures taken, recalling the famous photograph of the Lincoln conspirators "swinging in air under the hot July sun."[128]

123. Id. at 2952.
124. Id.
125. Id. at 2954.
126. Public Papers and Addresses of Franklin D. Roosevelt, 1942 Volume, 298 (New York: Harper & Bros., 1950).
127. Diary entry of August 4, 1942, by Oscar Cox, Papers of Oscar Cox, "Diaries and Related Material," Box 146, FDR Library.
128. Hassett, Off the Record with F.D.R., at 90.

Journalists assumed that the saboteurs would be executed either
by hanging or by firing squad. Lewis Wood of the *New York Times*
speculated that the executions would take place at an Army post
near Washington, D.C., perhaps Fort Belvoir, Fort Meade, or Fort
Myer, with the prisoners "meet[ing] their death in the early
dawn."[129] Reporters strained for clues. A story in the *Washington
Post* speculated about the significance of a load of lumber delivered
to Fort Myer "for no evident reason."[130] Was a hanging contem-
plated? Much of the public seemed to clamor for the death sentence. An article in *Life* magazine included a photo of eight Legion-
naires from Olyphant, Pennsylvania, who had volunteered to shoot
the saboteurs.[131]

Albert L. Cox, serving as jailer and custodian of the eight men,
learned from Judge Advocate General Cramer on August 4 that
Roosevelt would order the electrocution of six of the prisoners.[132]
Cox needed advance notice because he had to make changes in the
transformer, which was located on the street. Anyone watching
work performed on the transformer would have known what was
going to take place, but the prisoners could not see the street.

At a press conference on August 7, a reporter asked Roosevelt if
he had completed his review of the military trial. He replied, "Not
yet. Haven't finished reading it." Did he expect to finish that day?
Roosevelt: "I couldn't tell you. I don't know."[133] He dissembled.
The review was complete, the decision made, and the machinery for
execution under way. On August 8, Lewis Wood of the *New York
Times* discussed a published report of the previous day that six of
the men would be executed in the electric chair of the D.C. jail
within twenty-four hours.[134]

After learning that the executions were set for noon on August 8,

129. "Generals Consider Fate of Saboteurs," New York Times, August 2, 1942, at 16.
130. "Commission Gives Secret Spy Verdict to Roosevelt," Washington Post, August 4, 1942, at 4.
131. "The Eight Nazi Saboteurs," Life, July 13, 1942, at 33.
132. Albert L. Cox, "The Saboteur Story," Records of the Columbia Historical Society of Washington, D.C., 1957–1959, at 25.
133. Public Papers and Addresses of Franklin D. Roosevelt, 1942 Volume, at 326.
134. "Decision Is Near on Saboteur Band," New York Times, August 8, 1942, at 1.

Cox summoned six Army chaplains and had them enter the six cells that morning. Reporters waited outside in a drizzly rain. The procession to the death cells began at 10:00 a.m., with Haupt the first in the electric chair at one minute past noon. The last of the six was pronounced dead at 1:04 p.m.[135] The defense counsel were not informed of the decisions by the tribunal or Roosevelt and learned of the executions from the press.[136] The bodies were stored in individual compartments of the refrigeration room at the Walter Reed Hospital morgue and embalmed on August 10. At 6 p.m. on August 11, the bodies were placed in individual plain pine boxes and buried in Potters Field, Blue Plains, D.C.[137]

The Administration released this statement about Dasch and Burger: "There was a unanimous recommendation by the commission, concurred in by the Attorney General and the Judge Advocate General of the Army, that the sentence of two of the prisoners be commuted to life imprisonment because of their assistance to the Government of the United States in the apprehension and conviction of the others."[138] Dasch received a sentence of thirty years, and Burger was given life. The Administration reasoned that mercy for the two would encourage members of other espionage, sabotage, or fifth-column groups to turn against their colleagues and receive leniency.[139]

Roosevelt's mood on the evening of August 8 was recorded in notes taken by Rosenman's wife. Over dinner, Roosevelt told many stories about cases of executive clemency that he had worked on as governor of New York. The account gradually turned in a macabre direction, such as a French tale about a barber in Paris who had supplied a butcher with "veal" during the siege of 1870. Those who sampled the delicacy began to notice that some of the

135. Cox, "The Saboteur Story," at 25.
136. Mason, "Inter Arma Silent Leges," at 819.
137. Memo of August 14, 1942, from Walter Reed General Hospital to President Roosevelt, FDR Library.
138. "Six German Spies Put to Death in District Chair," Washington Post, August 9, 1942, at 1.
139. "2 Surviving Nazis Remain in Capital," New York Times, August 10, 1942, at 3.

barber's customers had not been seen for weeks. Roosevelt also told a story about an English general who had been killed in battle at New Orleans. To preserve him for the long trip back to England, they placed him in a barrel of rum. Roosevelt said that the body "would have been all right, but some of the crew got thirsty and used an auger on the way over."[140] Such was Roosevelt's effusive state of mind on the evening of August 8.

The Fate of Confederates

Initially, fourteen people were arrested for providing assistance to the saboteurs: eight in Chicago, six in New York City. The FBI searched the home of Herbert Haupt's parents in Chicago and found $2,550 in $50 bills placed in a brown envelope under the rug in his mother's bedroom. Hans Max Haupt knew that his son had arrived by submarine and had come to the country for the purpose of committing sabotage. His wife had also been fairly well informed. Both were taken into custody. Based on information given by the father, the FBI went to the home of Carl Eggert and found $900 in $50 bills in a small wooden box in a cabinet in the living room. Eggert later testified for the prosecution against Hans Haupt.[141]

In a trial that included his wife and two other couples (the Froehlings and Wergins), Hans Haupt was found guilty of treason and sentenced to death.[142] An appellate court voided the convictions, however, because the statements taken from Haupt and other defendants were inadmissible, separate trials should have been held, and there were deficiencies in the trial judge's charge to the jury.[143] In reversing the conviction, the appellate court indirectly or unwittingly

140. Samuel I. Rosenman, Working with Roosevelt, 352–54 (New York: Harper & Row, 1952).

141. "Fiance Describes Seeing Nazi Agent," New York Times, November 1, 1942, at 26.

142. "Six Found Guilty of Treason in Aiding German Saboteurs," New York Times, November 15, 1942, at 1; "Chicago Trio Get Death Penalty for Treason, Wives Prison Terms," New York Times, November 25, 1942, at 1.

143. United States v. Haupt, 136 F.2d 661 (7th Cir. 1943).

slammed the Supreme Court's decision in *Ex parte Quirin* for failing to protect the fundamental right of trial by jury:

Of the many rights guaranteed to the people of this Republic, there is none more sacred than that of trial by jury. Such right comprehends a fair determination, free from passion or prejudice, of the issues involved. The right is all-inclusive; it embraces every class and type of person. Those for whom we have contempt or even hatred are equally entitled to its benefits. It will be a sad day for our system of government if the time should come when any person, whoever he may be, is deprived of this fundamental safeguard. No more important responsibility rests upon courts than its preservation unimpaired. How wasted is American blood now being spilled in all parts of the world if we at home are unwilling or unable to accord every person charged with crime a trial in conformity with this constitutional requirement.[144]

Hans Haupt was later retried and sentenced to life imprisonment and fined $10,000.[145] The Supreme Court upheld that sentence in1947.[146] Ten years later, President Dwight D. Eisenhower commuted his sentence on the condition that he leave the country and be subject to reimprisonment if he returned. Haupt left prison and boarded a flight to Frankfurt, Germany.[147] His wife, found guilty of treason, received twenty-five years in prison and a fine of $10,000. Upon appeal, she was discharged but agreed to proceedings that would revoke her citizenship.

A search of the home of Herbert Haupt's uncle, Walter Froehling, uncovered a zipper bag on top of the mantel in the dining room. The bag appeared to be empty, but agents found $9,950 concealed in a secret compartment. Froehling admitted that Haupt had told him about reaching the United States by submarine and receiving training for sabotage. Also implicated were two close friends of the Haupts, Otto and Kate Wergin. Mr. Wergin had known that Herbert

144. Id. at 671.
145. Affirmed by the Seventh Circuit in United States v. Haupt, 152 F.2d 771 (7th Cir. 1946).
146. Haupt v. United States, 330 U.S. 631 (1947).
147. "Traitor to Quit Prison," New York Times, November 14, 1957, at 24; "Spy's Father Expelled," New York Times, November 15, 1957, at 14.

Haupt was acting as a German agent and had offered to help because he had been an "Intelligence man" in World War I. In the same trial as Hans Haupt, Froehling and Wergin were found guilty of treason and sentenced to death, but those convictions were reversed on appeal. Their wives were found guilty of treason and sentenced to twenty-five years in prison and fined $10,000. Later, Froehling and Wergin pleaded guilty to charges of misprision of treason (concealing an act of treason and failing to report it to authorities). They received sentences of five years each.[148] Their wives were released from prison.

Also in Chicago, Harry and Emma Jaques were arrested for hiding the money given them by Neubauer. Initially, Emma told FBI agents that she did not have the money. Finally, she showed them $3,600 in an envelope hidden in a five-gallon coffee can in the pantry off the kitchen. Her husband was not present as the agents counted seventy-two $50 bills. Jaques and his wife lost their citizenship and returned to Germany.[149]

The FBI picked up six others in New York City. Agents went to the home of Hermann Heinrich Faje and found $3,600 in $50 bills that Heinck had given him. Faje showed the agents the location of the money: between two sections of a radiator cover. The government indicted him for treason. Instead of that charge, he pleaded guilty to harboring Heinck and Quirin and was sentenced to five years in prison.[150] Prosecutors dropped the same charge against his wife.

Kerling's wife, Marie, knew from Helmut Leiner that her husband had returned to the United States, but she never saw him because he was arrested. Leiner, approved by the German High Command as a secret contact for the saboteurs, had met with Kerling and agreed to change some of the $50 bills to other currency. After Leiner was acquitted on the charge of treason, he was interned as a

148. "Two Get Terms of 5 Years in Nazi Plot Case; Appeal Saved Them from Death in the Chair," New York Times, July 23, 1944, at 9.

149. Rachlis, They Came to Kill, at 292.

150. "Pleads Guilty as a Spy," New York Times, December 5, 1945, at 3; "Saboteur Aide Jailed," New York Times, January 8, 1946, at 25.

dangerous alien enemy and subsequently reindicted for misprision of treason and violation of the Trading with the Enemy Act.[151] He pleaded guilty to illegal trading with the enemy— by helping Kerling change two $50 bills into smaller currency— and was sentenced to eighteen years in prison.[152]

Kerling's girlfriend, Hedwig Engemann, knew that he had arrived by submarine. There was also evidence that she planned to help him return to Florida to recover the explosives. Kerling, worried about the American money he had received in Germany, asked her to change a $20 bill and a $50, which she agreed to do. After her plea of guilty to misprision of treason, she was sentenced to three years in prison and fined $1,000.[153] Also arrested was Ernst Herman Kerkhof, who had been in close contact with Marie Kerling. His citizenship was revoked.[154] She also lost her citizenship and was ordered interned.

Anthony Cramer, after meeting with Thiel and Kerling, had agreed to take Thiel's $3,470 and deposit it in a bank. Found guilty of treason, he was sentenced to serve forty-five years in prison and pay a $10,000 fine.[155] In 1945, the Supreme Court held that the two acts on which his conviction of treason were based were insufficient to support a finding that he had given aid and comfort to the enemy.[156] He was later charged with violating the Trading with the Enemy Act and a presidential "freeze" order. After pleading guilty to the charge involving the Trading with the Enemy Act (because he had accepted the money from Thiel), he was sentenced to six years in prison.[157]

151. "Leiner Is Interned After Acquittal Ordered by Court in Treason Case," New York Times, December 1, 1942, at 1; "Leiner Reindicted for Aiding Treason," New York Times, December 5, 1942, at 17.

152. "Nazi's Friend Admits Trading with Enemy," New York Times, June 18, 1943, at 16; "Aide of Nazi Spy Gets 18-Year Term," New York Times, June 26, 1943, at 28.

153. "Saboteur's Friend, Guilty, May Aid U.S.," New York Times, November 5, 1942, at 14.

154. "Citizenship Revoked of Spies' Aide Suspect," Washington Post, July 19, 1942, at 6; "Twelve Face Trial as Saboteur Aides," New York Times, August 13, 1942, at 6.

155. Affirmed in United States v. Cramer, 137 F.2d 888 (2d Cir. 1943).

156. Cramer v. United States, 325 U.S. 1 (1945).

157. "Cramer Is Accused of Enemy Trading," New York Times, June 12, 1945, at 5; "Aide of Nazi Spies Gets 6-Year Term," New York Times, September 29, 1945, at 5.

In addition to these fourteen, others paid a price. William Wernecke had advised Herbert Haupt how to evade the draft, either by faking his medical exam or by joining a "church" and falsely claiming to be a conscientious objector. With that information in their hands, prosecutors went to a grand jury and indicted Wernecke for violating the Selective Service Act by assuming the role of a minister to evade the draft.[158] After his conviction, leading to five years' imprisonment and a $10,000 fine, he attempted an appeal to the U.S. Supreme Court. On February 7, 1944, the Court denied his petition for a writ of certiorari.[159]

Finally, the FBI followed up on one of the names written with secret ink on the handkerchiefs given to Dasch and Kerling: "Pas Krepper" (Pastor Emil Ludwig Krepper). Kerling had attempted to find Krepper at his New Jersey address but had been unsuccessful. Although Krepper never met with the Nazi saboteurs, the government indicted him in December 1944 for conspiring with Walter Kappe, sending coded messages to Germany, violating the Trading with the Enemy Act, and receiving a salary from the German government without notifying the Secretary of State that he was acting as a German agent.[160] His first trial ended with a finding of guilty for violating the sabotage and censorship statutes.[161] A month later, in a second trial, he was found guilty of violating the Trading with the Enemy Act and censorship laws.[162] He received twelve years in prison.

The military tribunal sat for nineteen days, from Wednesday, July 8, to Saturday, August 1 (with time off to allow the prosecution and defense

158. "Bundist Indicted in Draft," New York Times, November 14, 1942, at 6.
159. "Wernecke Guilty in Draft Case," New York Times, June 5, 1943, at 11; "Wernecke Fails to Gain Review," New York Times, February 8, 1944, at 34; Wernecke v. United States, 321 U.S. 771 (1944).
160. "Ex-Pastor Seized as Nazi Spy Aide," New York Times, December 21, 1944, at 1.
161. "Ex-Pastor Guilty in Sabotage Trial," New York Times, February 22, 1945, at 8.
162. "Krepper Guilty as Spy," New York Times, March 15, 1945, at 25.

counsel to visit Justice Roberts's farm on July 23 and to participate in proceedings before the district court and the Supreme Court from July 28 to 30). The tribunal reached a decision, as did President Roosevelt. Six of the Germans were executed. The Administration's job was complete. The Supreme Court's work had barely begun.

4

The Supreme Court Steps In

After Chief Justice Stone agreed to hear the case, both the prosecution and the defense hustled to write briefs and submit them to the Court. On July 27, reporters were notified to be at the Court at 5:45 p.m.[1] Upon arrival they learned that the Court would sit in special session on July 29 to hear the Nazi saboteur case. The announcement did not meet with universal approval. The public already disliked the length of the military trial. The *New York Times* reported that "all sides hope . . . that the Supreme Court would make short work of the move."[2] It surely did that. The *Los Angeles Times* objected to "a totally un-called-for" summoning of the Court in special session. "It should never have been dragged into this wartime military matter."[3]

On the evening of July 28, the district court turned down Royall's petition for a writ of habeas corpus, placing the matter before the Supreme Court. There followed two days of oral argument on July 29 and 30 and the Court's holding on July 31 that the military tribunal was properly constituted. In acting as quickly as it did, the Court could manage only a short per curiam. It would be almost three months before Stone and his colleagues could complete the full opinion, offering legal and constitutional *reasons* for the per curiam. Over that period, the Justices thrashed out language and arguments in an effort to satisfy not only legal standards but also political constraints.

1. "Supreme Court Is Called in Unprecedented Session to Hear Plea of Nazi Spies," New York Times, July 28, 1942, at 1.
2. Id. at 10.
3. "The Saboteurs Seek Civil Court Relief," Los Angeles Times, July 29, 1942, Part II, at 4.

Briefing the Case

How the Court prepared itself to hear the case is a wonder. Justices usually receive briefs in advance to give them time to study the issues, undertake independent research, and decide the sort of questions to put to counsel. Their law clerks supplement the record. In the Nazi saboteur case, the briefs submitted by the two sides are dated July 29, the same day that oral argument began. The highly compressed schedule probably explains why Chief Justice Stone decided to waive the Court's rule limiting each side to one hour. He gave the defense and prosecution whatever time they thought they needed. This agreement was good for the Justices, who needed time to understand issues of military law, which were rarely before the Court.

Argument by Defense Counsel. In their petition for a writ of certiorari, Dowell and Royall asked the Court to bring up the case pending in the appellate court "before judgment is given in that court."[4] Actually, they had not completed the paperwork to appeal the case from the district court to the D.C. Circuit. The incompleteness of the process is captured in this sentence, still to be filled out: "On July __, 1942, notices of appeal from the said orders were duly filed by the petitioners in the Court of Appeals for the District of Columbia."[5] They urged the Supreme Court to operate under its Rule 39, which allowed the Court to grant certiorari before judgment by an appellate court when the public interest would be promoted by prompt settlement of the questions involved. This issue of jurisdiction preoccupied the Justices at the start of oral argument.

As to the question presented, Dowell and Royall defined it this way: "whether the President of the United States may provide for the trial by military commission of offenses which are (with the exception of the charge of spying covered by Article of War 82)

---

4. "Petition for Writ of Certiorari to the Court of Appeals for the District of Columbia," reprinted in Landmark Briefs, at 296.

5. Id. at 299.

cognizable in the district or other appropriate courts of the United States, at a time when such courts of the United States are open and functioning regularly."[6] They also challenged Roosevelt's claim that he could deny the defendants access to civil courts except under such regulations as the Attorney General, with the approval of the Secretary of War, might prescribe. Their seven-page petition discussed other subsidiary questions.

In the much longer seventy-two-page brief in support of petitions for a writ of habeas corpus, Dowell and Royall identified the major issues. They posed two basic questions: (1) "May the Petitioners (six of whom are alien enemies) maintain this proceeding for Writ of Habeas Corpus?" and (2) "If so, are the Petitioners unlawfully restrained of their liberty?"[7] The brief challenged the validity of Roosevelt's proclamation creating the tribunal and his military order appointing the tribunal members.

Nothing in the four charges, they argued, justified Roosevelt's appointment of the tribunal. With regard to Charges II and III, claiming a violation of Articles of War 81 and 82, Dowell and Royall said that the defendants had not committed any act in a zone of military operations, and no proof existed of an effort to obtain military information. As to Charge I (the law of war), they could find nowhere "in the unpublished Rules of Land Welfare any such offense as is described in the specifications of the first Charge."[8] Moreover, they considered the law of war to be a species of international law analogous to common law and concluded that no principle "is better settled than the principle that there is no common law crime against the United States Government."[9] Crimes, they said, must be covered by a statute enacted by Congress. In short, the executive branch was attempting to usurp powers granted to Congress under the Constitution. To the extent a crime existed under the law of war, it would include the offenses of sabotage and espionage,

6. Id. at 297.
7. "Brief in Support of Petitions for Writ of Habeas Corpus," reprinted in Landmark Briefs, at 307.
8. Id. at 333.
9. Id. at 333–34.

which are treated in the statutes enacted by Congress and are "triable by the civil courts."[10] Charge IV, on conspiracy, was also covered by a congressional statute and "is not triable by a military commission."[11]

If the alleged criminal acts were not committed in a zone of military operations, civil courts were functioning "both in the localities in which the offenses were charged to have been committed and in the District of Columbia where the alleged offenses are being tried."[12] The brief denied that the tribunal could be justified on the ground of martial law, which was "a matter of fact and not a matter of Proclamation." No proclamation declaring martial law would be valid "unless the facts themselves support it."[13] Nothing in the President's proclamation or military order indicated a state of martial law, and nothing in the facts presented to the Court "justify martial law in the territory in question."[14]

Returning to the issue of interbranch conflict, Dowell and Royall concluded that President Roosevelt had no authority to issue his proclamation "in the absence of a statute giving him this authority."[15] No "inherent" presidential authority existed to justify the proclamation, they said, because the sole constitutional authority to define the "law of war" and to say what constitutes a criminal offense lay with Congress. Building on that point, they insisted that the constitutional right to suspend the writ of habeas corpus is found in Article I under the powers of Congress, not under Article II for the President.

Dowell and Royall flagged another issue: the Ex Post Facto Clause. The Constitution expressly prohibits Congress from passing an ex post facto law, which is a law that inflicts punishment on a person for an act that was not illegal at the time committed. Similarly, Congress cannot increase the penalty for a crime committed in

10. Id. at 334.
11. Id.
12. Id. at 335.
13. Id. at 340.
14. Id. at 341.
15. Id. at 342.

the past. Increased penalties apply only to future transgressions. Dowell and Royall pointed out that Roosevelt's proclamation had been issued after the commission of the acts charged against the defendants. The proclamation "is, therefore, ex post facto as to them."[16] Without the proclamation, the maximum penalty for sabotage in time of war could not exceed thirty years. In the case of espionage, the death penalty was not mandatory. Yet Roosevelt's proclamation allowed the death penalty if two-thirds of the tribunal so voted, even though Article of War 43 required a unanimous vote for a death sentence. Dowell and Royall further argued that Congress could not have passed legislation on July 2 increasing the penalty for the acts already committed. If the Constitution prohibited Congress from so acting, on what constitutional grounds could the President act?

Another "unusual feature" of Roosevelt's proclamation was its prohibition on judicial review unless the Attorney General, with the approval of the Secretary of War, allowed an exception.[17] How could the President, they asked, authorize an executive officer to waive a constitutional right? Other conflicts between Roosevelt's actions and the Articles of War were covered during oral argument, discussed in the next section.

Argument by Prosecutors. Responding to the petition for a writ of certiorari, Biddle and Cramer insisted that the defendants had "no capacity to sue in this Court or in any other court" because they were enemies of the United States.[18] Continuing, they argued that the Court had no jurisdiction to disturb the right of the Provost Marshal (Albert Cox) to hold the defendants in lawful custody "by virtue of the laws of war and the lawful orders of his superiors."[19]

Next, Biddle and Cramer submitted a longer brief of ninety-three pages to rebut the defendants' case. They argued that the German saboteurs were not entitled to have access to U.S. courts for

16. Id. at 343.
17. Id. at 344–45.
18. "Respondents's Answer to Petitions," id. at 393.
19. Id.

the purpose of obtaining writs of habeas corpus: "The great bulwarks of our civil liberties—and the writ of habeas corpus is one of the most important—were never intended to apply in favor of armed invaders sent here by the enemy in time of war."[20] Individuals ordered by the enemy to destroy American industries and lives "and the very existence of the Nation can hardly be in a position to claim constitutional rights, privileges, and immunities from the Nation which they seek to destroy."[21] Now that the defendants had brought a petition for a writ of habeas corpus to the Court to test the validity of their detention, the Justices "should find that they may legally be tried by the Military Commission set up for that purpose by the President."[22]

Biddle and Cramer argued that by "no stretch of interpretation" could *Ex parte Milligan* be applied to the defendants.[23] Lambdin Milligan did not wear the uniform of an armed force at war with the United States, he was continuously a resident of Indiana, and he did not cross through military lines and enter into a theatre of operations. The defendants, however, arrived on American shores in uniform, were residents of Germany, and "as agents of the German Government crossed our lines secretly in enemy warships for the purpose of committing hostile acts."[24]

Moreover, the charges against Milligan came at a time when invasions "gave their slow forewarning months in advance."[25] Modern warfare, in contrast, was swift and sudden. The theatres of operation of 1864 were not the theatres of operation of 1942: "Wars today are fought on the total front on the battlefields of joined armies, on the battlefields of production, and on the battlefields of transportation and morale, by bombing, the sinking of ships, sabotage, spying, and propaganda."[26] President Roosevelt, under his

20. "Brief for the Respondent," id. at 409.
21. Id. at 410.
22. Id. at 410–11.
23. Id. at 411.
24. Id.
25. Id.
26. Id.

constitutional oath to protect and defend the United States against enemies, "had the clear duty to meet force with force and to exercise his military authority to provide a speedy, certain and adequate answer, long prescribed by the law of war, to this attack on the safety of the United States by invading belligerent enemies."[27]

Biddle and Cramer noted that the Fifth Amendment of the Constitution, requiring presentment or indictment by a grand jury, did not apply to "cases arising in the land or naval forces." Thus, U.S. soldiers charged with military offenses had no right to insist on the protections of grand juries and civil trials. "It would be fantastic to extend such privileges to invading soldiers of the enemy."[28]

Having discussed the independent authority of the President to create military tribunals, Biddle and Cramer pointed out that Congress, by statute, had provided that these tribunals need not follow the procedures established for courts-martial. Belligerent enemies were therefore not entitled to some of the rights afforded by statute to members of U.S. forces, such as the right of peremptory challenges or the rule that requires a unanimous decision for a death sentence. Those rights and privileges "should not be granted to belligerent enemies who, in time of war, enter this country in order to destroy it by acts of war."[29]

Biddle and Cramer quoted from *Halsbury's Laws of England* to demonstrate that the writ of habeas corpus was a process for securing "the liberty of the subject," and that it was a prerogative writ by which the King had a right to inquire into the reasons why "any of his subjects" were deprived of their liberty.[30] The writ thus applies to *subjects of the nation,* not subjects of a country "with which we are at war, or who are subject to its orders." Halsbury specifically said that the writ of habeas corpus would not be granted "to an alien enemy who is a prisoner of war."[31] Those historic principles would deny "certain enemies" access to U.S. courts. Biddle and

27. Id. at 412.
28. Id. at 413.
29. Id.
30. Id. at 415
31. Id. at 416.

Cramer conceded that Halsbury's broad policy "has been relaxed in modern times in a very limited class of cases, to permit enemy nationals to have access to the courts in cases of civil litigation for the enforcement of pecuniary claims whenever the enemy nationals can be said to have been residing in the country with the license of the sovereign authority."[32] But this access to the courts, they said, is granted only to enemy nationals who lawfully reside in the United States, not to an enemy who unlawfully enters the country after war begins and with a hostile purpose. In oral argument, Biddle and Chief Justice Stone pursued this issue in greater detail.

Biddle and Cramer underscored their position that the judgment of trying the saboteurs lay solely with the President, and that neither Congress nor the judiciary could interfere with his decisions: "The President's power over enemies who enter this country in time of war, as armed invaders intending to commit hostile acts, must be absolute."[33] The proclamations and military orders issued by Roosevelt "were clearly within his power as Commander in Chief and Chief Executive, and were lawful acts of the sovereign—the Government of the United States—in time of war."[34] By the time the Court issued its full decision on October 29, it declined to endorse this ambitious theory of presidential power.

As to the alleged citizenship of Burger and Haupt, Biddle and Cramer argued that they had forfeited any claim to American citizenship by invading the United States as belligerent enemies. By actively aiding an enemy nation, their status had changed from U.S. citizen to enemy of the United States.[35] Dowell and Royall did not actively defend Burger's U.S. citizenship. They seemed to agree that he had lost that citizenship when he returned to Germany and joined its Army. Insisting that Haupt was a U.S. citizen, they lost that argument as well.

32. Id. at 416–17.
33. Id. at 423.
34. Id.
35. Id. at 426–27.

Nine Hours of Oral Argument

Without waiting for an appeal from the district court to the appellate court (the D.C. Circuit), the Supreme Court began oral argument at noon on July 29. All the Justices participated except for Frank Murphy, who thought that his status as an officer in the military reserves made it inappropriate for him to sit on the case. On military maneuvers when the emergency session was called, he returned to listen to the oral argument. William O. Douglas, scurrying across the United States from his home in Oregon, reached Washington in time for the second day of oral argument.

Disqualification? As a first order of business, Chief Justice Stone confronted the fact that his son, Lauson, was part of the defense team. If that involvement provided grounds for Stone not to participate in the case, he announced that he would "at once" disqualify himself. Biddle assured him that his son, although part of the defense at the military tribunal, "did not in any way participate in these habeas corpus proceedings" and urged Stone to sit in the case. Obviously this issue had been choreographed in advance. Stone asked the defense whether it concurred with Biddle's statement. Royall answered, "We do."[36]

Stone was not the only Justice with a cloud over his head. There were grounds for two others to disqualify themselves. Felix Frankfurter, accustomed to dropping in on the Administration to share his ideas on various matters of public policy, had already advised Secretary of War Stimson to try the Nazi saboteurs by a military commission. On the evening of June 29, over dinner, he told Stimson that the commission should be composed entirely of soldiers.[37]

James F. Byrnes had been serving as a de facto member of the Administration for the previous seven months, working closely with Roosevelt and Biddle on the war effort. Biddle had written a

36. Id. at 496–97.
37. Stimson Diary, June 29, 1942, at 131.

series of "Dear Jimmie" letters to Byrnes in late 1941 and early 1942, asking his advice on draft executive orders, a draft of the Second War Powers Bill, and other Administration proposals.[38] For some bills, Biddle asked Byrnes to "arrange for its introduction."[39] In his memoirs, Byrnes describes how in his capacity as Justice he called legislative leaders to secure their support for bills desired by the Administration and offered advice on various executive orders.[40] In late September, Roosevelt asked Byrnes to leave the Court and join the executive branch full-time. Byrnes resigned on October 3 to direct the Office of Economic Stabilization, before the Court issued its full opinion in *Ex parte Quirin.*

Jurisdictional Disputes. Chief Justice Stone, perhaps smarting from language in Roosevelt's proclamation that denied the eight Germans access to civil courts, put it straight to Biddle: "Does the Attorney General challenge the jurisdiction of this Court?" Biddle replied, "I do not, Mr. Chief Justice."[41] The question was direct, but the answer was not. As Biddle later explained to the Justices, he did not challenge the Court's jurisdiction to exercise its appellate jurisdiction over a writ of habeas corpus. He conceded that point. But he would make it clear later that he *did challenge* the Court's jurisdiction on other questions involved in the case, such as the President's exclusive authority to decide the manner of trying the defendants.[42] On that point Biddle did not waver. Basically, he consented to the Court reviewing the petition for a writ of habeas corpus, so long as it rejected it.

A separate jurisdictional issue concerned the Court's authority to take a case from the district court without first waiting for judgment from the appellate court, the D.C. Circuit. Frankfurter pressed the

38. Letters from Biddle to Byrnes, December 23, 1941 (one letter on a census bill and another on daylight saving), December 29, 1941, December 30, 1941, January 1, 1942, and January 10, 1942, Papers of James F. Byrnes, Special Collections, Clemson University.

39. Letter from Biddle to Byrnes, December 23, 1941, regarding a daylight saving bill.

40. James F. Byrnes, All in One Lifetime 148–54 (New York: Harper & Bros., 1958).

41. Landmark Briefs, at 498.

42. Id. at 583, 603, 604, 615, 635, 636.

point, asking both Royall and Biddle to state on what grounds the
Court could take the case directly from Judge Morris. Gamely, Royall did what an unprepared student in class might do: talk rapidly
and confidently around a question:

The Court is familiar with the statute which provides that the Supreme Court
may issue a writ of habeas corpus. That statute must, of course, be construed
consistently with the Constitution of the United States, which limits the jurisdiction of this Court to an appellate jurisdiction. To give the statute any
meaning at all, therefore, it must be construed as being a method of appeal
or a method of review. The ordinary methods of review are not included
within the writ of habeas corpus. Therefore the ordinary procedure . . . [43]

With Royall flailing away, hoping to strike something solid,
Frankfurter interrupted: "Why do you say that?" Royall tried
again. As he continued to struggle, a merciful Frankfurter tossed
this lifeline: "Could Congress provide that appeal from the district
court should only lie to the circuit court of appeals?" A relieved
Royall readily agreed that Congress could do that. Frankfurter took
the argument to the next step: "And the question is whether it
did?"[44] Royall hoped that citing *Ex parte Yerger* (1869) would
help, but Frankfurter pointed out that the case had no value because it had been decided before Congress created the appellate
courts in 1891. Frankfurter next asked Royall why he had not ap-
pealed Judge Morris's decision to the D.C. Circuit. Royall, re-
minding the Court that Morris had acted at 8 p.m. the previous
evening, acknowledged that the appeal "might have been perfected if we had had a little additional element of time."[45] He suggested that the Court agree to continue with the oral argument, and
he would take the procedural steps necessary to get the paperwork
to the D.C. Circuit.

Constitutionality of Tribunal. With jurisdictional issues set to the
side, Royall and the Justices focused on other disputes. He agreed

43. Id. at 498.
44. Id. at 499.
45. Id. at 500.

with the Justices that the Court was not being asked to determine the guilt or innocence of the defendants.[46] The sole issue was whether the Court would uphold or strike down the jurisdiction of the military tribunal. If its jurisdiction were denied, the government would have to take the case to a civil court and seek indictments from a federal grand jury.

The Court then explored whether the country was in a state of martial law. Chief Justice Stone asked Royall, "Under the Constitution, the President, either with or without the authority of Congress, may declare martial law and enforce martial law?" Royall agreed that the President had that potential power, and under martial law "properly and constitutionally declared . . . some form of military court would try it."[47] Stone thought that Roosevelt's proclamation might have declared martial law because it referred to the eight Germans as taking part in "an invasion or predatory incursion." Royall disagreed, stating that martial law "ordinarily is a territorial matter and not a matter dependent upon the character or conduct of the individual."[48]

Royall admitted that the government could have shot the eight men as they landed, "because they were apparently invading our country," but once they entered the country and were apprehended, they could not be tried before a military tribunal and executed. Justice Jackson pursued that point: "That is like the case of a criminal whom you might shoot at in order to stop the commission of a crime; but when he has committed it, he has a right to trial?"[49] Agreeing with that analogy, Royall finally had an opportunity to tick off his central propositions:

First, the petitioners, including the aliens, are entitled to maintain this present proceeding.

Second, the President's Proclamation, which assumes to deny the right of the petitioners to maintain this proceeding, is unconstitutional and invalid.

46. Id. at 511.
47. Id. at 513.
48. Id. at 514.
49. Id. at 515–16.

Third, the President's Order, which assumes to appoint the alleged Military Commission, is unconstitutional and invalid.

Fourth, the President's Order, relating to the alleged Military Commission, is contrary to statute and, therefore, illegal and invalid.

Fifth, the petitioners are entitled to be tried by the civil courts for any offenses which they may have committed.[50]

Justice Byrnes asked about the status of the eight men who had entered the country and changed from military uniforms to civilian clothes. If Hitler and seven generals landed from a submarine on the banks of the Potomac River in Washington, D.C., and discarded their uniforms, would they be entitled "to every right you have discussed in the application for a writ of habeas corpus and to require an indictment by a grand jury under the Constitution?" Royall conceded that his argument "would have to carry that fact, and does."[51] Justice Reed interjected: "Does that mean that every spy is entitled to be heard by the civil courts?" Royall answered in the negative, "because there is a specific statute which deals with spies," later adding that he thought the statute was valid.[52] Frankfurter crystallized the point: "What you are saying is that that which Congress can take out of the constitutional provisions by statute, the President as Commander-in-Chief cannot take out of civil statute by military proclamation?" Royall replied, "That is correct."[53]

Oral argument clarified another point. Stone asked whether the Court could correct errors of a military court, assuming that the tribunal had authority to act. Royall answered, "You cannot do that, sir. In other words, habeas corpus, of course, is not a method of reviewing the facts."[54] He was not bringing the case to the Court to determine guilt, innocence, or procedural errors. The sole issue was whether the tribunal had jurisdiction to hear and decide the case, or whether the case should be sent to a civil court. With that issue settled, the Court took a recess after the first two hours of argument.

50. Id. at 516.
51. Id. at 520.
52. Id. at 521.
53. Id. at 522.
54. Id. at 528.

Presidential Authority. Following the break, the Justices and Royall focused on the President's authority to create a military commission. Stone presented this hypothetical: "Assuming they came in
bearing arms and were prepared to use them, has the President constitutional authority to appoint a commission to try and condemn
them and, in connection with that, to suspend the writ?" Royall denied that the President had any constitutional authority to suspend
the writ in the absence of an express statute. Congress "is the only
one that can authorize the suspension of the writ under the first Article and under the Fifth Amendment."[55]

Royall also challenged the validity of the first charge because it
relied on the "law of war," which he called "a sort of common international law." He told the Court, "there is a serious question as to
whether there is any such offense as the violation of the Law of
War."[56] Instead of trying to divine the meaning and intent of the law
of war, nowhere specifically written down, the better course was to
rely on the statutory Articles of War and other enactments of Congress: "There are Congressional enactments in the form of criminal
statutes covering the acts these people might have committed,
under the stipulation; and we think it a very cogent circumstance
that, the Congress having legislated over the entire field, and the
civil courts functioning in this territory, it is unnecessary and contrary to our theory of government to appoint a military commission
to do what Congress has clearly indicated should be done by the
criminal courts."[57]

Frankfurter wondered whether there might be "some discretion"
in the Commander in Chief Clause to create a military commission.
Royall conceded that this grant of presidential power included
"some element of discretion," but not the power to create military
commissions when civil courts are open and operating.[58] Frankfurter continued to press the point, leading to a technical analysis of
whether the eight Germans were in a "theatre of operations" or a

55. Id. at 535.
56. Id. at 536.
57. Id. at 537–38.
58. Id. at 539–40.

"zone of operations." As this line of questioning continued, Royall suggested that Frankfurter was advancing the "total war theory." Frankfurter denied that he had used those words, but Royall replied, "No, you have not, sir. But the total war theory is that anything that affects the war effort is a part of the war. There has got to be some limit on that, or we have very few constitutional guarantees left when we go to war."[59]

Conflicts with Congressional Statutes. Royall insisted that Congress possessed the constitutional authority to legislate on military courts and military tribunals, and that any action by the President contrary to statutory standards would be invalid. He read this language from the 38th Article of War:

> The President may, by regulations, which he may modify from time to time, prescribe the procedure, including modes of proof, in cases before courts martial, courts of inquiry, military commissions, and other military tribunals, which regulations shall, in so far as he shall deem practicable, apply the rules of evidence generally recognized in the trial of criminal cases in the district courts of the United States. Provided, that nothing contrary to or inconsistent with these Articles shall be so prescribed.[60]

Royall charged that Roosevelt's proclamation and military order violated the Articles. Instead of complying with Article 38, which directed the *President* to prescribe the rules of procedure, Roosevelt had transferred that function to the military commission. Making matters worse, the commission issued few rules in advance. On July 7, the day before the trial began, the tribunal adopted a three-and-a-half-page, double-spaced statement of rules. This document dealt primarily with the sessions being closed to the public, the taking of oaths of secrecy, the identification of counsel for the defendants and the prosecution, and the keeping of a record. Only eight lines referred to rules of procedure: disallowing peremptory challenges, allowing one challenge for cause, and then this

59. Id. at 548.
60. Id. at 550.

concluding language: "In general, wherever applicable to a trial by Military Commission, the procedure of the Commission shall be governed by the Articles of War, but the Commission shall determine the application of such Articles to any particular question."[61] For the most part, then, the commission made up the rules as the trial went along. Royall told the Justices that this arrangement "could change the requirement from two strikes to three strikes after we got at the bat." His analogy would have been stronger had the change been from three strikes to two.

Another inconsistency was that the Articles required unanimity for a death penalty, but Roosevelt's proclamation allowed a two-thirds majority. Royall insisted that the 38th Article had to govern, because Roosevelt had specifically cited it in his military order appointing the commission members, the prosecution, and the defense counsel. It seemed clear to Royall that the procedures adopted by the President for a military commission "must follow the *Manual of Courts-Martial* and that no procedure can be prescribed for the Military Commission that does not follow the Articles of War and as construed in the *Manual for Courts-Martial*."[62]

For other inconsistencies between Roosevelt's military commission and the Articles of War, Royall pointed to the review procedure in Article 46. Before the President could act, the trial record of a general court-martial or a military commission had to be referred to a staff judge advocate or the Judge Advocate General for review. Also, Article 50½ provided for examination by a board of review. Yet Roosevelt's proclamation required the trial record of the military commission to come directly to him as the final reviewing authority. This inconsistency was compounded by another change. Instead of having the Judge Advocate General function in an independent capacity to review the adequacy of a military trial, Roosevelt had placed him in the role of prosecutor with the Attorney General.[63]

61. "Rules Established by the Military Commission Appointed by Order of the President of July 2, 1942," at 3–4, McCoy Papers.

62. Landmark Briefs, at 551.

63. Id. at 557–61.

Debating Ex parte Milligan. In internal documents, the Justice Department prepared analyses to discredit *Ex parte Milligan.* Writing to Biddle, Oscar Cox referred to *Milligan* as a "famous old case" and a "well-worn decision," accepting the view of critics who charged that the "broad dicta of the majority opinion" could never stand "the strain of actual war."[64] Yet apparently age alone did not make a case "old" or "well-worn." The Justice Department had no difficulty in singling out the *Prize Cases,* decided three years before *Milligan,* as a "much wiser precedent."[65]

In oral argument, Royall and Biddle squared off on the application of *Milligan* to the eight saboteurs. Royall told the Justices that both the majority and the minority opinions in that case "fully sustain our view." He acknowledged that the reach of *Milligan* could be limited to U.S. citizens but insisted that his defendants were entitled to trial before a criminal court.[66] In rebuttal, Biddle said that alien enemies had no right to sue or to enter U.S. courts "under these circumstances, both because of the President's proclamation and because of the statutes governing the case, and also because of the very ancient and accepted common law rule that such enemies have no rights in the courts of the sovereign with which they are enemies." The issue, Biddle said, was not whether the defendants were U.S. citizens or aliens. Royall conceded that Burger had lost his citizenship by joining the Nazi Army, and Biddle maintained that Haupt had forfeited his citizenship as well. To Biddle, the essential issue was not U.S. citizenship but the status of the defendants as enemies of the United States.[67]

Chief Justice Stone suggested a different cut. Instead of citizens versus noncitizens, or citizens versus alien enemies, he drew this distinction: "We recognize that ordinarily the courts are not open to an alien enemy plaintiff, but we also recognize that courts are open to a

64. Memo from Cox to Biddle, July 6, 1942, at 6, "German Saboteurs, Trial of (I)," Papers of Oscar Cox, Box 61, FDR Library.
65. Id. at 7.
66. Landmark Briefs, at 564–65.
67. Id. at 565.

man charged with an offense to defend himself."[68] Stone had flagged
that issue earlier when he and Biddle engaged in this dialogue:

> STONE: I mean under the statute as it stands today is there any question
> that an alien enemy, if he is accused of a crime, may defend himself?
> BIDDLE: No.
> STONE: Or in a civil suit may defend the suit?
> BIDDLE: No, but I think a statute could be passed under which other
> jurisdiction could be taken for the trial of any alien.
> STONE: No such statute has been passed.
> BIDDLE: No such statute has been passed.[69]

Biddle returned to *Milligan,* claiming that nothing in that case af-
fected the saboteurs except "a certain dictum . . . which seemed to
me profoundly wrong."[70] He argued that *Milligan* should be limited
to its particular circumstances. In that case, a congressional statute
of 1863, requiring the President to notify courts of persons held
under suspension of the writ of habeas corpus, had not been followed. It was on that ground, Biddle said, that Milligan's petition
for a writ of habeas corpus should have been granted.[71] In that sense,
Milligan was a matter of not following a statute and did not represent a citizen's general right to a civil trial when the courts were
open and operating. He told the Justices that "war today is so swift
and so sudden and so universal that it would be absurd to apply a
doctrine like the doctrine in the *Milligan* case."[72] The first day of oral
argument, consuming five and a half hours, ended at 6 p.m.

The Rights of Aliens. The Court met the next day at noon, with Justice Douglas sitting on the dais with his colleagues. Biddle opened
up an issue that had been only tangentially explored: Which branch
of government decides the rights of aliens? He made it clear that the
Constitution gave aliens no right of access to U.S. courts. To the

68. Id. at 569.
69. Id. at 566–67.
70. Id. at 573.
71. Id. at 575.
72. Id. at 580.

extent that such rights existed, they came from statutes enacted by Congress: "The question seems to me to be: What is the law with respect to aliens? For that law we look to the Act of 1917, as brought back in this war; we look to the Act which I quoted yesterday, the Act of 1798; and we look to the President's Proclamation."[73]

Could a presidential proclamation overturn a policy that Congress had established by statute? Biddle seemed to regard Roosevelt's proclamation as merely *confirming* congressional policy, not acting against it. He said that "there is nothing in the statute which permits them to come into court without the proclamation."[74] Justice Reed checked his understanding: "Without the proclamation." Biddle continued: "Therefore, I think that at common law and under the statutes to which I have referred they have no right; but to close any possibility, the President signed a proclamation." Thus, Roosevelt's proclamation merely confirmed what Congress had established by law. Stone pressed for clarification: "Assume that your opponents are right in saying that there is no jurisdiction in a military court to try the case of these people on its merits. Would a proclamation change that? Biddle: "Oh, I think not."[75] In other words, if Congress decided that there was no jurisdiction in a military court to try aliens on the merits, a presidential proclamation would not change that.

As he saw the way this dialogue was developing, Biddle told Stone that "perhaps I answered your question a little too quickly." In the two paragraphs below, Biddle starts by claiming that the war power is exercised jointly by Congress and the President, but toward the end he argues that in some instances a President as Commander in Chief could act in ways that even Congress could not control:

I think it is conceivable, as I just pointed out in the opening of this argument, that the powers of waging war, of raising armies, of making regulations governing the armies, and the powers of the President as Executive

73. Id. at 606.
74. Id. at 607.
75. Id.

and Commander-in-Chief—these powers in the Constitution express all the powers of the Executive and of the Legislative.

It is conceivable that if there were no statute, or even if the statute, as in the *Milligan* case, specifically provided that these men under certain circumstances could not be tried by a military tribunal, the President, in the exercise of his great authority as the Commander-in-Chief during the war and in the protection of the people of the United States, might issue such proclamations which no Congress could set aside, because it might be considered that those proclamations were a proper expression of his executive power; but, as I said yesterday—[76]

At that point, Chief Justice Stone cut him off: "We do not have to come to that?" With its hands more than full, the Court saw no reason to decide whether the President possessed some kind of exclusive power that could not be controlled by Congress (or the judiciary). Biddle agreed: "You do not have to come to that."[77] Still, Biddle could not let it go. Frankfurter later told him that he had made one concession, "precisely within the scope of Colonel Royall's argument, when you said, 'except, of course, as modified by Congress.'" Biddle was reluctant to give ground:

Perhaps I narrowed that too much. I have always claimed that the President has special powers as Commander-in-Chief. It seems to me, clearly, that the President is acting in concert with the statute laid down by Congress. But I am glad you have brought up the point, because I argue that the Commander-in-Chief, in time of war and to repel an invasion, is not bound by a statute.[78]

This formulation quickened the interest of Justice Roberts: "That is to say that the Articles of War bind him sometimes and sometimes they do not?" Biddle conducted a partial retreat: "No. I do not say that, Mr. Justice Roberts. I say that it is perfectly clear that in this case there is no conflict." Roberts double-checked his understanding: "You mean, his action does not conflict with the Act of Congress?" Biddle: "Yes, sir." Roberts accepted that argument as

76. Id.
77. Id. at 608.
78. Id. at 636.

"perfectly understandable" but said that he had understood Biddle to say that if the President "acted in conflict with the Acts of Congress it still was all right." Biddle tried again:

I do not think I went quite as far as that. I think we could imagine situations where the President could act, in repelling an invasion, irrespective of an Act of Congress. He must have some constitutional power that Congress cannot interfere with, as Commander-in-Chief. I think it is unnecessary for me to argue it here, first, because he has acted clearly under the Articles of War, and secondly, whether or not that procedure is followed is not for this Court to go into.[79]

As to any possible conflict between Roosevelt's action and the Articles of War, Biddle said that Article 46 "is the only case whether there is a doubt."[80] Royall, entering the argument at that point, identified difficulties not only with Article 46 but also with Articles 38, 48, and 50½.[81] After two hours of oral argument, the Court took a thirty-minute recess. When the Justices returned, they entered into a diffuse discussion about the Articles, with neither Royall nor Biddle nor the Justices shedding much light on how the Articles applied to the President. Had Roosevelt acted in concert with the Articles or at variance with them? The next hour and a half of argument, wandering from one issue to the next, added little clarity. Royall made one of the few concrete points by insisting that the "Law of War" could not create offenses punishable in the courts, whether military or civil. No one, he said, "can create an offense in the absence of express Congressional enactment. The Constitution requires that." On the same point: "I say there is no Law of War in absence of a statute."[82]

Either two full days of debate had dulled the minds of the participants or they were simply unprepared to tackle, clarify, and dispose of questions that cried out for answers. After oral argument on July 30, the Justices met in conference to discuss the best course

79. Id.
80. Id. at 637.
81. Id. at 637–38.
82. Id. at 652, 658.

of action.[83] Many of the issues raised during those two days of oral argument would have to be revisited over the next three months as Chief Justice Stone worked on a draft opinion to explain the Court's reasons.

The Per Curiam

At noon on July 31, Chief Justice Stone read a short per curiam opinion that upheld the military tribunal. Defense lawyers carried the papers from the D.C. Circuit to the Supreme Court only a few minutes before Stone spoke. The petition for certiorari was not filed in the Court until 11:59 a.m. on July 31. One minute later the Court convened, granted certiorari, and announced its per curiam decision.[84] Through these procedural niceties, the Court was able to act on "writs of certiorari to the United States Court of Appeals for the District of Columbia." In granting certiorari, the Court denied motions for leave to file petitions for writs of habeas corpus and affirmed the decision of the district court.

In announcing its decision, the Court said that it was acting "in advance of the preparation of a full opinion which necessarily will require a considerable period of time for its preparation and which, when prepared, will be filed with the Clerk." A quick per curiam was necessary because the military tribunal had been put on hold while Royall and Dowell explored the relief available in the civil courts. The per curiam allowed the tribunal to complete its work. In the terse ruling, the Court held that the military commission was lawfully constituted and that the defendants were held in lawful custody and had not shown cause for being discharged by writ of habeas corpus.[85]

83. Frankfurter's "Notes taken at conference," July 30, 1942, Felix Frankfurter Papers, Part III, Reel 43, LC (hereafter Frankfurter Papers).

84. General Myron C. Cramer, "Military Commissions: Trial of the Eight Saboteurs," 17 Washington Law Review & State Bar Journal 247, 253 (1942).

85. Ex parte Quirin, 63 S.Ct. 1–2 (1942). The per curiam is also reproduced in a footnote in Ex parte Quirin, 317 U.S. 1, 18–19 (1942).

Stone's Draft

Having disposed of the issue with two days of oral argument and a brief per curiam, the Court still had to produce its "full opinion." That responsibility fell on Chief Justice Stone. The complexity of his task was heightened on August 8 with the execution of six of the saboteurs. Clearly, nothing in Stone's opinion for the Court could now cast doubt on the per curiam. He did not want the Court's reputation damaged by concurrences and dissents. Particularly in this case, it was crucial to hold the Court together.

It would have been easier for Stone to draft the decision in Washington, D.C., with easy access to legal materials at the Court's library. Trying to write from his summer home in Franconia, New Hampshire, proved very difficult. On August 1, he wrote to his law clerk, Bennett Boskey, asking for the draft of the per curiam, which he had forgotten to bring with him. Stone expressed concern at the version he had seen in the *New York Times,* which included reference to Articles of War 46 and 50½. He thought he had omitted that paragraph. (He had.) Stone knew that the full opinion "must deal with them and will have a sour look" if the men had been executed "without the kind of review required by 50½." Stone expressed frustration with the analyses thrown at him by the government and the defendants: "Both briefs have done their best to create a sort of a legal chaos."[86]

In a letter to Boskey on August 5, Stone said that he had written as much as he could but still had not received some of the documents he needed. He planned to work on the draft in New Hampshire and return to Washington about September 11 or 12 to "finish the job in good style." He needed help on issues related to the law of war and the Articles of War: "We may also come finally to the question whether we or the Commission & President should construe articles 46 & 50½ etc."[87] For six of the saboteurs, "coming to that issue" would be a little late.

---

86. Letter from Harlan Fiske Stone to Bennett Boskey, August 1, 1942, Papers of Harlan Fiske Stone, Box 69, LC (hereafter Stone Papers).
87. Letter from Stone to Boskey, August 5, 1942, Stone Papers.

By August 9, Stone appeared to have settled on a strategy. What he needed from Boskey were materials "to show that petitioners are unlawful belligerents in the International Law and Law of War sense, which would bring them within the jurisdiction of Military Tribunals, which the Commander in Chief under the Constitution & Article XV of the Articles of War may set up for their trial independently of the 5 & 6 amendments, as such their case is distinguished from that of Milligan who was not a beligerant [sic] or waging war because not associated with the armed forces of the enemy and acting under their direction."[88] That thought appeared later in the October 29 decision.

On August 16, Stone thanked Boskey for sending a memo that analyzed the legal and constitutional issues. Stone had completed the first draft and sent eighteen pages to his secretary. He decided to revise the law of war section "in light of your memo," although what he had written paralleled Boskey's effort "very closely." He was troubled by what Boskey had said about the use of uniforms. "I have written the opinion on the assumption that the law is the other way as I think it ought to be." Stone ended his note by saying that he was "laid up" with lumbago.[89] To Frankfurter, later in the month, he admitted that he thought he could "disregard" the pain as he did with other ailments. Recalling Justice Holmes's warning that "You can't fool God," he added that you can't fool "the devil either."[90]

Stone wrote to Frankfurter on September 10 that he found it "very difficult to support the Government's construction of the articles [of war]." He said, it "seems almost brutal to announce this ground of decision for the first time after six of the petitioners have been executed and it is too late for them to raise the question if in fact the articles as they construe them have been violated." Only after the war, he said, would the facts be known, with release of the

88. Letter from Stone to Boskey, August 9, 1942, Stone Papers.
89. Letter from Stone to Boskey, August 14, 1942, id.
90. Letter from Stone to Frankfurter, August 29, 1942, Frankfurter Papers.

trial transcript and other documents to the public. By that time, Dasch and Burger could raise the question successfully, which "would not place the present Court in a very happy light."[91]

Articles 46 and 50½. By mid-September, Stone's initial draft had circulated to the other Justices, and he was back in Washington responding to their comments. Writing to Frankfurter on September 16, he said he planned to put out a memorandum opinion "which will present to the Court alternative views, one of which will have to be followed." He would accompany that opinion with another memo "which will indicate the embarrassments to which the Court will be exposed whichever procedure is adopted." Stone shared with Frankfurter his concerns about the legislative construction of the review procedures set forth in Article of War 46.[92]

In a memo for the Court on September 25, Stone explored the meaning of Articles of War 38, 43, 46, and 50½. Their construction, he said, raised a question of "some delicacy and difficulty." In presenting the case at conference, immediately following oral argument on July 30, he had expressed "doubts as to the construction of those Articles and stated that if it were necessary to decide the point I should not be able to decide without further investigation; that in my opinion it would be unnecessary to decide it, and in fact would be improper to do so since there were no facts disclosed on the record of the habeas corpus proceedings which drew in question the construction of the Articles." Stone reasoned that Roosevelt's order had not foreclosed review by the Judge Advocate General or by a staff judge advocate. He thought that the other Justices had agreed with his approach, "since the Conference did not attempt to pass upon the construction of the Articles in question or to say that the contentions made by petitioners with respect to them were wrong." Thus, in preparing the per curiam, he included one paragraph stating that the Court did not pass upon the construction of Articles 46

91. Letter from Stone to Frankfurter, September 10, 1942, Frankfurter Papers.
92. Letter from Stone to Frankfurter, September 16, 1942, Stone Papers.

and 50½ in the absence of a decision by the military commission or action of the President requiring their construction.[93]

The Court decided to strike that paragraph from the per curiam. Stone was now "in doubt as to how the Court intended the opinion to be written—whether (a) it should decline to pass upon the Articles in question on the ground that their construction was not before us or, in the alternative (b) it should construe the Articles contrary to the contention of the petitioners." He said that the first ground "was and is a perfectly tenable legal ground of decision, wholly consistent with the per curiam." Still, he noted this "embarrassment": "the announcement that we have left the construction of Articles 46 and 50½ undecided is now made for the first time after six of the petitioners have been executed and when it is too late to raise the question in their behalf." There were many facts the Court did not know. It did not know if the decision of the military tribunal had been unanimous or what method of review the President had adopted. If the two survivors renewed their applications for habeas corpus, "their petitions would necessarily lack any factual basis for the construction of the Articles in question." Even if the Court knew the facts, "the knowledge would not alter the record on which we acted and on which our opinion must be written."[94]

Looking down the road, Stone saw great risks for the Court: "whenever the facts do become known, as they ultimately will, the survivors, if still in prison, will be in a position to raise the question. If the decision should be in their favor it would leave the present Court in the unenviable position of having stood by and allowed six to go to their death without making it plain to all concerned—including the President—that it had left undecided a question on which counsel strongly relied to secure petitioners' liberty."[95]

The second alternative—construing the statutes against the petitioners' contentions—also carried substantial risks. To Stone, the Court might be deciding "a proposition of law which is not free

93. "Memorandum re Saboteur Cases," September 25, 1942, at 1, Stone Papers.
94. Id. at 1–2.
95. Id. at 2.

from doubt upon a record which does not raise it." In short, the Court would be rendering an advisory opinion. He saw no justification for writing a "legal essay" on the meaning of Articles 46 and 50½. To present the issues fully to the Justices, he prepared a memo opinion with alternative endings designated Memorandum A and Memorandum B. The first declined to pass upon the construction of the Articles; the second ventured a construction. He acknowledged that Memorandum B troubled him because he could find no basis in the record to write an opinion on the subject, and he was "reluctant" to see the Court write an advisory opinion.[96]

The Court decided to avoid the pitfalls of Memorandum B. The full decision released on October 29 concluded that the secrecy surrounding the trial made it impossible for the Court to judge whether Roosevelt's proclamation and order violated or were in conflict with the Articles of War.[97] Having issued the per curiam, the Justices were in no position to look too closely at whether Roosevelt had acted inconsistently with the Articles of War. In the words of Alpheus Thomas Mason, "Their own involvement in the trial through their decision in the July hearing practically compelled them to cover up or excuse the President's departures from customary practice."[98]

Keeping a United Front

Institutionally, it was important for the Court to issue a unanimous opinion and avoid any concurrences that might raise doubts about the per curiam, the full opinion, or the execution of six men. Stone did what he could to keep any daylight from shining through vulnerable spots in the decision. He wanted to stick to fundamental points and discourage his colleagues from offering supplemental views. He did not want them wandering down unnecessary alleyways that might embarrass the Court.

96. Id.
97. Ex parte Quirin, 317 U.S. 1, 46–47 (1942).
98. Mason, "Inter Arma Silent Leges," at 826.

Nevertheless, Robert Jackson worked on several drafts of a concurrence. An early version, double-spaced, begins: "I concur in the opinion in so far as it finds these prisoners properly to be in military custody and that the President might lawfully set up a military commission for their trial. I think our functions end with that finding." He deleted these sentences: "I suppose no one doubts that they could have properly been shot without trial or even warning as they were landing. They were then in uniform, and that under international law of war gave them certain privileges such as that of surrender and of receiving treatment agreed upon for prisoners of war." These passages remained: "By casting aside their uniforms and concealing their identity, they lost those rights which they might otherwise have claimed under the laws of war. Even as enemies go, these were outlaw enemies. Because they thus forfeited their standing as lawful enemies they certainly did not gain rights to bring the President's orders and the action of military authorities into the Courts for examination and judgment."[99]

Not satisfied with that, Jackson continued to underscore the impropriety of giving enemy belligerents the privilege of entering civil courts "to claim protection of the majestic generalities of the Constitution designed to safeguard the rights of our inhabitants."[100] He saw nothing in congressional statutes that might admit of such a construction. He now ventured into territory that Stone had indicated during oral argument was off bounds: speculating about a form of presidential power that could not be controlled by either Congress or the courts. Jackson wrote, "We should not only be slow to find that Congress unwittingly had done such a thing, but even if it had clearly done so we would have a serious question of the validity of any such effort to restrict the Commander in Chief in the discharge of his Constitutional functions."[101]

Hugo Black asked his law clerk, John P. Frank, to comment on Jackson's argument that there was "serious question" whether Con-

---

99. Undated draft, at 1, Papers of Robert H. Jackson, Box 124, LC (hereafter Jackson Papers).

100. Id. at 1(a).

101. Id.

gress could ever restrict the President in his capacity as Commander in Chief. To Frank, that position was "completely and outrageously wrong." It was what Biddle, during oral argument, "was trying to get out of this Court—an expression of complete executive authority." Frank did not agree that the President's position as Commander in Chief "gives him authority to over-ride express acts of Congress," and he worried that any deference by the Court to presidential powers in military affairs would likely strengthen executive power in the domestic field, including control over farm prices.[102]

In a memo to Stone on October 2, Black expressed uneasiness about two points: the vague realm of the law of war, and the excessive scope given to military tribunals. While he acknowledged that Congress had the constitutional authority to declare "all violations of the Laws of War to be crimes against the United States," he seriously questioned whether it could constitutionally confer jurisdiction to try "*all* such violations before military tribunals." He did not want to say that "every violation of every rule of the Laws of War" between nations would subject every person living in the United States to the jurisdiction of military tribunals. He was comfortable only with declaring that the eight Germans could be tried by a military tribunal "because of the circumstances and purposes of their entry into this country as a part of the enemy's war forces." By limiting the decision in this fashion, the Court would leave *Milligan* "untouched." However, to subject everyone in the United States to trial by military tribunal "for every violation of every rule of war which has been or may hereafter be adopted between nations among themselves, might go far to destroy the protections declared by the *Milligan* case." Black was convinced that the law of war "may well cover certain acts for which persons cannot be tried by military tribunals under the Constitution even though we might be compelled to admit that the conduct charged actually constituted violation of the Law of War."[103]

Stone tried to limit the reach of the Court's decision. In particular,

102. "Ex parte Quirin: The Jackson Memo," undated memo from Frank to Black, Papers of Hugo LaFayette Black, Box 269, LC (hereafter Black Papers).

103. Memo from Black to Stone, October 2, 1942, Black Papers.

he did not want to go down the road traveled by Jackson. On October 23, he proposed language that the Court would later adopt in its essentials:

We hold therefore that the President did not vary the procedure of the Commission in any respect from that which Congress has either expressly or impliedly directed. Since his action does not conflict with any law of Congress, it would be gratuitous for us to inquire whether Congress could restrict the authority of the Commander in Chief to discipline enemy belligerents, or to consider the role of the courts if he were to ignore such restriction.[104]

Toward the end of his draft concurrence, Jackson developed a point that he made in subsequent years. He said that he pressed his views "because in the long run it seems to me that we have no more important duty than to keep clear and separate the lines of responsibility and duty of the judicial and of the executive-military arms of government." Combining the two, he said, "is the end of liberty as we in this country have known it." He reasoned that the Court could protect the rights of U.S. citizens only if it steered clear of interfering with military decisions affecting the enemy: "If we are uncompromisingly to discountenance military intervention in civil justice, we would do well to refuse to meddle with military measures dealing with captured unlawful enemy belligerents."[105]

The more Jackson worked on his concurrence, the longer it got. Possibly reacting to criticism that his separate opinion fractured the unity of the Court, he changed the initial sentence from "I concur in the opinion" to "I agree with the opinion."[106] The drafts progressed from typewritten versions to page proofs. As late as October 23, he titled the page proofs a "memorandum" rather than a concurrence.[107] Still, whatever he called it, a separate statement is a separate statement. Constantly nudged by his colleagues, Jackson withdrew the memo.

104. "Memorandum for the Conference," October 23, 1942, signed H.F.S., Jackson Papers.
105. Undated draft, at 4, Jackson Papers.
106. Undated draft, attached to a printer's version of the opening page, showing the parties to the case, Jackson Papers.
107. Papers of William O. Douglas, Box 77, LC.

Jackson was not the only Justice interested in penning independent views. Frankfurter also had a "memorandum" in page proofs, agreeing with Stone's position as to why Memorandum B was defective. To go in that direction, said Frankfurter, was to risk a "brutal" announcement after six of the Germans had been executed. On the first page of this memo, Frankfurter wrote with assurance that "there can be no doubt that the President did *not* follow" Articles of War 46 through 53. On page three, he stated that he had "not a shadow of doubt" that Roosevelt "did not comply with Article 46 *et seq.*" But then he fudged the issue by saying that "either he did comply or he did not."[108] Stone had to stay on the alert to keep memos of this quality from being published.

Frankfurter used back channels to maximize his influence. In a letter to Justice Reed on August 26, he discussed Articles of War 46, 48, and 50½. He then added a dig at Stone's competence, suggesting that the Chief Justice might see the light with the help of his law clerk, Bennett Boskey: "I spelled it all out in case the C.J. should continue in the fog of pedantic unreality on this phase of the case. I hope & assume not. I have not sent him this memo—in the hope that he will discover the plain meaning & common sense of it (with Boskey's help) and then tell us all about it."[109] Years later, Douglas said that it was "unfortunate the court took the case." While it was "easy to agree on the original per curiam, we almost fell apart when it came time to write out the views."[110]

F.F.'s Soliloquy

At some point in October, when it looked like the Court might fragment with separate statements, Frankfurter wrote a peculiar document he called "F.F.'s Soliloquy." He sent it to his colleagues with

108. "Memorandum of Mr. Justice Frankfurter, *In re Saboteur Cases,*" id.
109. Letter from Frankfurter to Reed, August 26, 1942, at 2, Papers of Stanley Reed, Margaret I. King Library, University of Kentucky.
110. William O. Douglas, The Court Years, 1939–1975, at 138–39 (New York: Vintage Books, 1981).

this note attached: "Dear Brethren: This goes to you with affection and respect. F.F."[111] It might have been his attempt to inject some humor, but it also seemed designed to insert a backbone in any colleague who threatened to backslide. The memo was especially bizarre because it represented a conversation between Frankfurter and the saboteurs, six of whom were dead. In that sense, "soliloquy" was indeed the proper word, because Frankfurter was engaging in a monologue, not a dialogue. Moreover, the memo abandoned any pretense of judicial objectivity and balance. To Frankfurter, Roosevelt had the undoubted power to create the commission, and all else was needless talk injurious to the country.

The memo began by expressing discomfort about what he had heard in a recent conference: "After listening as hard as I could to the views expressed by the Chief Justice and Jackson about the *Saboteur* case problems at the last Conference, and thinking over what they said as intelligently as I could, I could not for the life of me find enough room in the legal differences between them to insert a razor blade." And now he was in receipt of Jackson's memo (a potential concurrence) "expressing what he believes to be views other than those contained in the Chief Justice's opinion." What could possibly be the legal dispute between them, Frankfurter wondered. He concluded that mere verbal differences were being used to express "intrinsically identic [*sic*] views about the governing legal principles." Puzzled by these exchanges, he wanted to express his own views about the saboteur case and thought he could do that "with least misunderstanding" by putting his thoughts "in the form of a dialogue—a dialogue between the saboteurs and myself as to what I, as a judge, should do in acting upon their claims."

SABOTEURS: Your Honor, we are here to get a writ of habeas corpus from you.

F.F.: What entitles you to it?

111. Presumably, Frankfurter sent the document to each Justice. I am relying on the copy in the Jackson Papers. Frankfurter's memo has been expertly analyzed by Michal Belknap, "Frankfurter and the Nazi Saboteurs," Yearbook 1982: Supreme Court Historical Society 66–71.

S: We are being tried by a Military Commission set up by the President although we were arrested in places where, and at a time when, the civil courts were open and functioning with full authority and before which, therefore, under the Constitution of the United States we were entitled to be tried with all the safeguards for criminal prosecutions in the federal courts.

F.F.: What is the answer of the Provost Marshal to your petition?

S: The facts in the case are agreed to in a stipulation before Your Honor.

F.F.: (after reading the stipulation): You damned scoundrels have a helluva cheek to ask for a writ that would take you out of the hands of the Military Commission and give you the right to be tried, if at all, in a federal district court. You are just low-down, ordinary, enemy spies who, as enemy soldiers, have invaded our country and therefore could immediately have been shot by the military when caught in the act of invasion. Instead you were humanely ordered to be tried by a military tribunal convoked by the Commander-in-Chief himsel[f], and the verdict of that tribunal is returnable to the Commander-in-Chief himself to be acted upon by himself. To utilize a military commission to establish your guilt or innocence was plainly within the authority of the Commander-in-Chief. I do not have to say more than that Congress specifically has authorized the President to establish such a Commission in the circumstances of your case and the President himself has purported to act under this authority of Congress as expressed by the Articles of War. So I will deny your writ and leave you to your just deserts with the military.

S: But, Your Honor, since as you say the President himself professed to act under the Articles of War, we appeal to those Articles of War as the governing procedure, even bowing to your ruling that we are not entitled to be tried by civil courts and may have our lives declared forfeit by this Military Commission. Specifically, we say that since the President has set up this Commission under the Articles of War he must conform to them. He has certainly not done so in that the requirements of Articles 46–50½ have been and are being disregarded by the McCoy tribunal.

F.F.: There is nothing to that point either. The Articles to which you appeal do not restrict the President in relation to a Military Commission set up for the purpose of and in the circumstances of this case. That amply disposes of your point. In lawyer's language, a proper construction of Articles 46–50½ does not cover this case and therefore on the merits you have no rights under it. So I don't have to consider whether, assuming Congress has specifically required the President in establishing such a Commission to give you the procedural safeguards of Articles 46–50½, Congress would have gone beyond its job and taken over the business of the President as Commander-in-Chief in the actual conduct of a war. You've done enough mischief already without leaving the seeds of a bitter conflict involving the President, the courts and Congress after your bodies will be rotting in lime. It is a wise requirement of courts not to get into needless rows with the other branches of the government by talking about things that need not be talked about if a case can be disposed of with intellectual self-respect on grounds that do not raise such rows. I therefore do not propose to be seduced into inquiring what powers the President has or has not got, what limits the Congress may or may not put upon the Commander-in-Chief in time of war, when, as a matter of fact, the ground on which you claim to stand—namely, the proper construction of these Articles of War—exists only in your foolish fancy. That disposes of you scoundrels. Doubtless other judges may spell this out with appropriate documentation and learning. Some judges would certainly express their views much more politely and charmingly than I have done, some would take a lot of words to say it, and some would take not so many, but it all comes down to what I have told you. In a nutshell, the President has the power, as he said he had, to set up the tribunal which he has set up to try you as invading German belligerents for the offenses for which you are being tried. And for you there are no procedural rights such as you claim because the statute to which you appeal—the Articles of War—don't apply to you. And so you will remain in your present custody and be damned.

In the closing paragraph, Frankfurter laid bare his feelings: a sense of patriotism in wartime that placed national unity above constitutional concerns. Some of the "very best lawyers" he knew were in battles under way in the Solomon Islands, in service in Australia, chasing enemy submarines in the Atlantic, or performing their duty in military aircraft. What would they think, in putting their lives on the line, if a unanimous opinion of the Court was clouded by "internecine conflict about the manner of stating that result"? If the Court issued not only the decision for the majority but also concurrences, they would say, "What in hell do you fellows think you are doing? Haven't we got enough of a job trying to lick the Japs and the Nazis without having you fellows on the Supreme Court dissipate the thoughts and feelings and energies of the folks at home by stirring up a nice row as to who has what power when all of you are agreed that the President has the power to establish this Commission and that the procedure under the Articles of War for courts martial and military commissions doesn't apply to this case [?]" He counseled against getting involved in "abstract constitutional discussions." The better course was not to be "too engrossed in your own interest in verbalistic conflicts because the inroads on energy and national unity that such conflict inevitably produce, is a pastime we had better postpone until peacetime."

The October 29 Decision

The Court's full opinion touched on one of the motives for hearing the case in an extraordinary summer session: "In view of the public importance of the questions raised by their petitions and of the duty which rests on the courts, in time of war as well as in time of peace, to preserve unimpaired the constitutional safeguards of civil liberty."[112] In this manner the Court hoped to send the following message: even when Presidents in proclamations attempt to deny defendants access to civil courts, the Supreme Court will be there to insist on exercising its independent review.

The message was largely a fiction, even though fictions sometimes serve a purpose. There was never a likelihood that the Court would exercise judicial review in any but the most limited sense. It would not scrutinize the record of the tribunal, attempt to take the case away and transfer it to a civil court, or reverse President Roosevelt. Still, the Court wanted to indicate that the judiciary is not irrelevant in time of war, even if during World War II the Court largely acquiesced to the political branches. After being stiff-armed by Roosevelt, it decided to declare its rights and assert its identity as a coequal, independent branch.

This claim of judicial independence and a capacity to check presidential abuses would look increasingly hollow as the Court upheld other military actions, such as the curfew and detention of

112. Ex parte Quirin, 317 U.S. 1, 19 (1942).

Japanese-Americans. The willingness of Justices to fold in the face of constitutional violations did great damage to the prestige of the Court, prompting several Justices to rethink judicial behavior in time of war. Looking back at the Nazi saboteur case, the Court carried water for the Administration and would do so again. Instead of functioning as an independent institution, it served more as a wing of the White House. No one looking at the record of the Court during World War II could take seriously its claim that the courts, "in time of war as well as in time of peace," would "preserve unimpaired the constitutional safeguards of civil liberty."

With great delicacy, the Court acknowledged that oral argument on July 29 and 30 had proceeded while the defendants "perfected their appeals" from the district court to the D.C. Circuit.[113] Through this language, the Court disposed of the fact that the papers from the D.C. Circuit reached the Court only a few minutes before it handed down its decision on July 31.

The Court chose not to address certain questions (often a wise course of action). Did Haupt lose his U.S. citizenship because he "elected to maintain German allegiance and citizenship"?[114] The Court found it unnecessary to decide that issue. It also made it clear that it was not concerned "with any question of the guilt or innocence of petitioners."[115] Their detention and trial could not be set aside by courts "without the clear conviction that they are in conflict with the Constitution or laws of Congress constitutionally enacted."[116]

The Court began with some fundamentals: "Congress and the President, like the courts, possess no power not derived from the Constitution."[117] It then itemized the war powers conferred upon Congress and the President and the Articles of War enacted by Congress, including the Articles that recognize military tribunals to punish offenses "against the law of war not ordinarily tried by court-

113. Id.
114. Id. at 20.
115. Id. at 25.
116. Id.
117. Id.

martial."[118] These statutes reflected the constitutional authority of Congress under Article I to "define and punish . . . Offences against the Law of Nations."[119]

By taking this approach, the Court decided that President Roosevelt had exercised authority "conferred upon him by Congress," as well as whatever authority the Constitution granted the President.[120] Could the President act independently under his interpretation of inherent or implied power, even to the extent of acting contrary to congressional policy as expressed in statute? The Court decided not to go there: "It is unnecessary for present purposes to determine to what extent the President as Commander in Chief has constitutional power to create military commissions without the support of Congressional legislation."[121] While accepting the great power of Congress to define the law of war, it also recognized that Congress might decide not to enact specific rules for every occasion: "Congress has the choice of crystallizing in permanent form and in minute detail every offense against the law of war, or of adopting the system of common law applied by military tribunals so far as it should be recognized and deemed applicable by the courts. It chose the latter course."[122]

The Court distinguished between "lawful combatants" (uniformed soldiers) and "unlawful combatants" (enemies who enter the country in civilian dress). The former, when captured, are detained as prisoners of war. The latter are subject to trial and punishment by military tribunals.[123] Although the Court declined to address Haupt's status as a U.S. citizen, it made it clear that U.S. citizenship of an enemy belligerent "does not relieve him from the consequences for a belligerency which is unlawful because in violation of the law of war."[124] A U.S. citizen who associates himself with the

118. Id. at 27.
119. Id. at 28.
120. Id.
121. Id. at 29.
122. Id. at 30.
123. Id. at 30–31.
124. Id. at 37.

military arm of an enemy government and enters the United States
for the purpose of committing hostile acts is an enemy belligerent
"within the meaning of the Hague Convention and the law of
war."[125] Such was the status of Haupt.

The Court was unimpressed with the argument that the defendants did not actually commit or attempt to commit any act of sabotage or enter the theatre or zone of active military operations. The
defendants were enemy belligerents because they passed military
and naval lines in civilian dress with hostile purpose. "The offense
was complete when with that purpose they entered."[126] Their conduct excluded them from such constitutional protections as jury trials or access to civil courts.

Turning to *Milligan,* the Court distinguished the facts of that
case from the Nazi saboteurs' situation. Milligan was a U.S. citizen
who had resided in Indiana for twenty years; he did not reside in
any of the rebellious states and was not an enemy belligerent entitled to POW status or subject to the penalties imposed on unlawful
belligerents.[127] He was a "non-belligerent, not subject to the law of
war."[128] The Court declined to define with "meticulous care" the
"ultimate boundaries" of military tribunals to try persons charged
with violating the law of war. It was enough for the Court to say that
the defendants were "plainly within these boundaries."[129]

Did the President's proclamation and order conflict with Articles
of War 38, 43, 46, 50½, and 70? The Court held that the secrecy surrounding the trial and proceedings before the tribunal "will preclude
a later opportunity to test the lawfulness of the detention."[130] So
much for the Court's earlier claim that it was there in time of war or
peace "to preserve unimpaired the constitutional safeguards of civil
liberty."

Other questions were left unaddressed. "We need not inquire

125. Id. at 37–38.
126. Id. at 38.
127. Id. at 45.
128. Id.
129. Id. at 46.
130. Id. at 47.

whether Congress may restrict the power of the Commander in Chief to deal with enemy belligerents."[131] The Court was unanimous in deciding that the Articles in question "could not at any stage of the proceedings afford any basis for issuing the writ."[132] Although unanimous on that conclusion, the Court was divided on the legal reasons: "a majority of the full Court are not agreed on the appropriate grounds for decision." Some Justices believed that Congress did not intend the Articles of War to govern a presidential military tribunal convened to try enemy invaders. Others concluded that the military tribunal was governed by the Articles of War, but that the Articles in question did not foreclose the option selected by President Roosevelt.[133]

In a memo written on the same day that the decision was issued, Biddle summarized for Roosevelt the main conclusions reached by the Court. In two and a half pages, Biddle covered the main points. In noting that the Court had distinguished *Milligan*, Biddle made this sweeping claim: "Practically then, the Milligan case is out of the way and should not again plague us."[134] The Court did indeed distinguish *Milligan* and narrowed some of its dicta, but the case was hardly "out of the way." There has been substantial criticism of the procedures used by the Court in deciding *Ex parte Quirin*. After World War II, the judiciary began to take steps to revive the constitutional principles announced in *Milligan* and to place restraints on military tribunals and courts-martial. When President George W. Bush authorized a military tribunal on November 13, 2001, he specifically excluded its application to U.S. citizens. The reconsideration of *Quirin* is addressed in the next chapter.

131. Id.
132. Id.
133. Id.
134. Memo from Biddle to Roosevelt, October 29, 1942, at 2, OF3603 in "OF3584-OF3617," Box 1, FDR Library.

5

Rethinking Tribunals

The Court received great credit for meeting in special session to consider the legal rights of the Nazi saboteurs. The haste with which the Court moved, however, left doubts in the minds of some whether justice had been served. Were nine hours of oral argument an impressive display of judicial independence and the rule of law or largely show? A repeat German sabotage effort late in 1944, with the submarine this time discharging its passengers off the coast of Maine, led to heated debate within the Administration on the proper organization and procedures for military tribunals. As a result, significant changes were instituted.

Judicial rulings during World War II, particularly the Court's approval of the curfew and detention of Japanese-Americans, provided stark evidence of a Court forfeiting its reputation as the guardian of constitutional rights. With the war over, the Court began to reassert itself and place restrictions on military tribunals and courts-martial, gradually restoring the right of U.S. citizens to jury trials in civil court. Matters changed abruptly with the September 11, 2001, terrorist attacks on the World Trade Center and the Pentagon, followed by President George W. Bush's authorization two months later of trials by military tribunal. Issues seemingly long settled were once again actively debated.

Evaluations of Quirin

The 1942 trial of the German saboteurs drew praise in many quarters as an impressive display of American standards of justice.

There was much in the way of self-congratulation. An editorial in the *Washington Post* said that "Americans can have the satisfaction of knowing that even in a time of great national peril we did not stoop to the practices of our enemies."[1] After the Court completed two days of oral argument, a *Post* editorial discovered an "element of the sublime in the action of the Chief Justice in calling this extraordinary session of the court."[2] The *New York Times* predicted that the full opinion, "which will be made public later on, will go into our constitutional history beside the Milligan decision, delivered in 1866."[3] For those who wondered why the men were tried instead of being placed against a wall and shot, the *Times* took the high ground: "We had to try them because a fair trial for any person accused of crime, however apparent his guilt, is one of the things we defend in this war."[4] The *New Republic* wrote: "It is good to know that even in wartime and even toward the enemy we do not abandon our basic protection of individual rights." With this decision Americans could broadcast to the world "that they have invoked the rule of law even in the case of enemy saboteurs."[5]

The initial public reaction consisted of patriotic—almost giddy—breast-beating. One of the few to express skepticism about the trial was Norman Cousins of the *Saturday Review of Literature*. Just as there was no need for a summary execution, there was "similarly no need to make a farce out of justice, when everyone knew at the very start of the trial what the outcome would be. If the saboteurs *actually had a chance,* it would be different, but they didn't; we knew it, and they knew it."[6] A similar remark came from constitutional scholar Edward S. Corwin, who viewed the Court's October 29 opinion as "little more than a ceremonious detour to a

---

1. "Justice Is Done," Washington Post, August 9, 1942, at 6.

2. "Habeas Corpus," Washington Post, July 31, 1942, at 12.

3. "Motions Denied," New York Times, August 1, 1942, at 10.

4. "They That Take the Sword," New York Times, August 9, 1942, at 8.

5. "The Saboteurs and the Court," New Republic, August 10, 1942, at 159.

6. "The Saboteurs," Saturday Review of Literature, August 8, 1942, at 8 (emphasis in original).

predetermined end."[7] John P. Frank, who had clerked for Justice Black in 1942, remarked that the Court "sent the defendants to their deaths some months before Chief Justice Stone was able to get out an opinion telling why."[8]

Wiener's Analysis. Frankfurter was sufficiently troubled by the decision to ask Frederick Bernays Wiener, an expert on military justice, to express his views on *Quirin.* Wiener prepared three analyses: the first on November 5, 1942, the next on January 13, 1943, and the final on August 1, 1943. Each one found serious deficiencies with the Court's work.

The first analysis credited the Court for taking "the narrowest—and soundest—ground" in holding that the eight saboteurs were "war criminals (or unlawful belligerents) as that term is understood in international law" and that, "under established American precedents extending back through the Revolution, violators of the laws of war were not entitled, as a matter of constitutional right, to a jury trial."[9] Wiener thought the decision was helpful in clarifying certain aspects of *Milligan* and for "putting citizenship in its proper perspective in relationship to war offense." Still, he criticized the Court for creating a "good deal of confusion as to the proper scope of the Articles of War insofar as they relate to military commissions." Weaknesses in the decision flowed "in large measure" from the Administration's disregard for "almost every precedent in the books" when it established the military tribunal.[10]

Before turning to those defects, Wiener complimented the Court for confronting some of the "extravagant dicta" in the majority's opinion in *Milligan.* He also thought the Court was on target in treating Haupt's citizenship as irrelevant in deciding the tribunal's jurisdiction to try him for a violation of the law of

7. Edward S. Corwin, Total War and the Constitution 118 (New York: Alfred A. Knopf, 1947).
8. John P. Frank, The Marble Palace: The Supreme Court in American Life 249 (New York: Alfred A. Knopf, 1972).
9. "Observations of Ex parte Quirin," signed "F.B.W.," at 1, Frankfurter Papers.
10. Id.

war.[11] Yet Wiener "parted company" with the Court because of what he considered its careless or uninformed handling of the Articles of War. The Court said that Article 15 saved the concurrent jurisdiction of military commissions.[12] Wiener argued that the legislative history of Article 15 demonstrated that it was intended as a *restriction* on military commissions, which had extended their authority to offenses punishable by courts-martial. During the Civil War, military commissions had repeatedly and improperly assumed jurisdiction over offenses better handled by courts-martial.[13]

Wiener emphasized that Congress may limit the jurisdiction of military tribunals by statute, and it seemed to him "perfectly plain that the Articles of War are applicable to military commissions to the extent that they in terms purport to apply to such tribunals." The fact that President Roosevelt appointed the commission did not give it a free charter. If the President appointed a general court-martial, it would still be subject to the provisions of the Articles of War. Presidential appointment did not make a tribunal "immune from judicial scrutiny."[14] Passages from the *Digest of Judge Advocate General's Opinions* showed that military tribunals are subject to restrictions just like courts-martial: "the rules which apply in these particulars to general courts-martial have almost uniformly been applied to military commissions."[15]

Especially potent is the way Wiener analyzed Article of War 46, which required that the trial record of a general court-martial or military commission be referred for review to the staff judge advocate or the Judge Advocate General. It seemed "too plain for argument" that Article 46 required "legal review of a record of trial by military commission before action thereon by the reviewing authority; that the President's power to prescribe rules of procedure did not permit him to waive or override this requirement; that he did in fact do so;

11. Id.
12. Ex parte Quirin, 317 U.S. 1, 28 (1942).
13. "Observations of Ex parte Quirin," at 3–4.
14. Id. at 4.
15. Id. at 5.

and that he disabled his principal legal advisers by assigning to them the task of prosecution."[16] It would be difficult to craft a more sweeping condemnation.

Were Roosevelt's actions justified under his powers as Commander in Chief, or by invoking implied or inherent executive authority? Not to Wiener: "I do not think any form of language, or any talk about the President's inherent powers as Commander in Chief, is sufficient to justify that portion of the precept, which, in my considered judgment, was palpably illegal."[17] Having identified these legal and constitutional violations, Wiener nevertheless concluded that "not even this flagrant disregard of AW 46 was sufficient to justify issuance of the writ" of habeas corpus. The issue before the Court was whether the saboteurs were in lawful custody, not whether they could be sentenced "without benefit of the advice of staff judge advocate." Royall had conceded in oral argument that the Court was not being asked to correct procedural errors. Wiener made the same point: "Errors in procedure, and the question of petitioner's guilt or innocence, are beyond the scope of inquiry on habeas corpus to a military tribunal."[18]

Wiener flagged other problems. Military commissions were normally appointed by War Department Special Orders, not by presidential proclamation or military order. He found only one precedent of using the Judge Advocate General of the Army as prosecutor, and it was one "that no self-respecting military lawyer will look straight in the eye: the trial of the Lincoln conspirators." Even in that sorry precedent, "the Attorney General did not assume to assist the prosecution."[19]

Wiener thought the saboteurs could have been "perfectly well" tried either by commissions appointed by the Commanding Generals of New York and Florida or by a military commission operating under the limitations of a general court-martial. The trial record, he

16. Id. at 8.
17. Id.
18. Id. at 9.
19. Id.

said, should have been reviewed by the Judge Advocate General before being sent to the President.[20] Under Roosevelt's proclamation and military order, that was impossible. When the German saboteurs arrived in November 1944 and were apprehended, they were tried along the lines suggested here by Wiener.

Two months later, in a second letter to Frankfurter, Wiener reported that he had "been digging a little deeper into the AW 46 matter, and while in a sense it is tied up with AW 50½, it is necessary to discriminate between the various portions of AW 50½." As to Article 46, a commanding general "may disregard his staff JA's advice, but he is bound to have it before him before he acts."[21] Under Article 50½, the President may also disregard his staff judge advocate, but "there is this exception, that in presidential cases the President's approval is final—there is no one to review after him as there is in the case of subordinate commanders."[22] To Wiener, the conclusion seemed "inescapable that AW 46 and ¶2 of AW 50½ read together require that the record of trial by a military commission appointed by the President must go to the B/R [Board of Review] and the JAG [Judge Advocate General]." There was no basis to contend that a presidential military commission is subject to procedures that vary from ordinary military commissions "except where statute makes it so." The Constitution vested authority in Congress, not the President, to "define and punish . . . Offences against the Law of Nations." Both Article 46 and paragraph 2 of Article 50½ "imposed such limitations" on the President.[23]

Writing a third time, on August 1, 1943, Wiener reiterated his position that the eight Germans, coming into U.S. territory in civilian clothes as unlawful belligerents, had no constitutional right to a jury trial. What of the Administration's argument—accepted by the Court—that Article of War 15 provided an affirmative direction by Congress that offenses against the law of war should be tried by

20. Id. at 9–10.
21. Letter from Wiener to Frankfurter, January 13, 1943, at 1, Frankfurter Papers.
22. Id. at 2.
23. Id. at 3.

military commissions? To Wiener, the legislative history of Article 15 (which first appeared in 1916) made it "at least doubtful whether Congress had any affirmative legislation in mind." Brig. Gen. Enoch H. Crowder, Judge Advocate General of the Army from 1911 to 1923, explained to Congress in 1916 that Article 15 had been included to clarify two points: that it was not the intent in legislating on courts-martial to exclude trials by military commissions, and that military commanders "in the field in time of war" had the option of using either one:

A military commission is our common-law war court. It has no statutory existence, though it is recognized by statute law. As long as the articles embraced them [a number of persons included in AW 2 who are also subject to trial by military commission] in the designation "persons subject to military law" and provided that they might be tried by court-martial, I was afraid that, having made a special provision for their trial by court-martial, it might be held that the provision operated to exclude trials by military commission and other war courts; so this new article was introduced. . . .

It just saves to these war courts the jurisdiction they now have and makes it a concurrent jurisdiction with courts-martial, so that the military commander in the field in time of war will be at liberty to employ either form of court that happens to be convenient.[24]

Wiener omitted from the second paragraph Crowder's concluding sentence: "Both classes of courts have the same procedure."[25] Congress did not intend military tribunals to dream up their own rules and regulations. When Congress created the Judge Advocate General in 1862, it directed his office to receive, "for revision, the records and proceedings of all courts-martial and military commissions."[26] The review procedure was identical for both. However, Roosevelt's proclamation authorized the military tribunal to depart from those procedural safeguards whenever it decided it was appropriate or necessary.

24. Letter from Wiener to Frankfurter, August 1, 1943, at 1–2, citing S. Rept. No. 130, 64th Cong., 1st Sess. 40 (1916), Frankfurter Papers (material in brackets added by Wiener).
25. S. Rept. No. 130, 64th Cong., 1st Sess. 40 (1916).
26. 12 Stat. 598, §5 (1862).

The letters from Wiener must have had an impact on Frankfurter. In 1953, when the Court was considering whether to sit in summer session to hear the espionage case of Ethel and Julius Rosenberg, someone recalled that the Court had sat in summer session in 1942 to hear the saboteur case. Frankfurter wrote, "We then discussed whether, as in *Ex parte Quirin,* 317 U.S. 1, we might not announce our judgment shortly after the argument, and file opinions later, in the fall. Jackson opposed this suggestion also, and I added that the *Quirin* experience was not a happy precedent."[27] In an interview on June 9, 1962, Justice Douglas made a similar comment: "The experience with *Ex parte Quirin* indicated, I think, to all of us that it is extremely undesirable to announce a decision on the merits without an opinion accompanying it. Because once the search for the grounds, the examination of the grounds that had been advanced is made, sometimes those grounds crumble."[28]

Law Reviews. The articles that first appeared in law journals were generally brief descriptions of *Quirin,* offering little in the way of analysis, judgment, or evaluation.[29] Somewhat more perceptive were two articles written by Robert E. Cushman in 1942, although he wrote quickly and without access to many of the facts that would become public within a few years.[30] Other short treatments were published during the first year, offering little more than description.[31] An article in the *Harvard Law Review* did note that as a

27. "Memorandum Re: *Rosenberg* v. *United States,* Nos. 111 and 687, October Term 1952," June 4, 1953, at 8, Frankfurter Papers, Harvard Law School, Part I, Reel 70, LC.

28. Conversation between Justice William O. Douglas and Professor Walter F. Murphy, June 9, 1962, at 204–5, Seeley G. Mudd Manuscript Library, Princeton University.

29. E.g., "Notes: Jurisdiction of Military Tribunals," 37 Illinois Law Review 265 (November–December 1942); George T. Schilling, "Saboteurs and the Jurisdiction of Military Commissions," 41 Michigan Law Review 481 (December 1942).

30. Robert E. Cushman, "Ex parte Quirin et al.—The Nazi Saboteur Case," 28 Cornell Law Quarterly 54 (November 1942); Robert E. Cushman, "The Case of the Nazi Saboteurs," 36 American Political Science Review 1082 (December 1942).

31. Charles Cheney Hyde, "Aspects of the Saboteur Cases," 37 American Journal of International Law 88 (January 1943).

result of "certain powers vested exclusively in Congress by the Constitution, it would seem that Congress has the basic power to create military commissions."[32]

Of potentially greater interest are the articles written by participants. General Cramer discussed his experience in handling the prosecution with Biddle. However, he wrote before the full opinion was released on October 29 and covered only the bare facts that had already been made public. Yet he offered this compliment: "In the gravest times of war, our highest court convened quickly during midsummer in extraordinary session to hear and weigh the arguments of counsel for petitioners and Government, in a manner characteristic of its spirit and traditions."[33]

An article by Col. F. Granville Munson, who assisted Cramer during the trial, was also limited to matters of public record and written in advance of the full opinion. He did make this distinction between courts-martial and military tribunals: "A court-martial has no authority to make rules for the conduct of its proceedings. Its procedure is rather rigidly prescribed in the *Manual for Courts-Martial* (1928) which, by Executive order of November 29, 1927, is prescribed for the government of all concerned."[34] He also pointed out that a general court-martial must have as one of its members a "law member" (an officer of the Judge Advocate General's Department, if available), who would rule on the admissibility of evidence. The military tribunal for the saboteurs lacked a law member.[35] In "several important particulars" (such as peremptory challenges), the rules followed by the tribunal "were at variance with the statutory provisions for general courts-martial."[36]

[handwritten margin note: court martial vs military tribunal]

---

32. Note, "Federal Military Commissions: Procedure and 'Wartime Base' of Jurisdiction," 56 Harvard Law Review 631, 639 (January 1943).

33. General Myron C. Cramer, "Military Commissions: Trial of the Eight Saboteurs," 17 Washington Law Review and State Bar Journal 247, 253 (November 1942).

34. F. Granville Munson, "The Arguments in the Saboteur Trial," 91 University of Pennsylvania Law Review 239, 240 (November 1942).

35. Id.

36. Id. at 240–41.

A more extensive treatment, written after the full opinion, appeared in an article by Cyrus Bernstein. He still promoted the misconception that the FBI had found Dasch, and not the other way around: "As he fell afoul of the F.B.I. special agents' net, one of the men made a full confession."[37] Bernstein highlighted the ex post facto issue in Roosevelt's proclamation, which increased the maximum penalty of sabotage from thirty years to death: "Congress could not have passed an *ex post facto* law of that tenor; Congress could not have authorized the President to issue such a proclamation."[38] Bernstein also pointed to a conflict of interest for Biddle. The proclamation authorized the Attorney General, with the approval of the Secretary of War, to make exceptions to the prohibition against remedies or proceedings in the civil courts, yet Biddle also served as prosecutor.[39] Similarly, Bernstein noted that Cramer's participation with the prosecution eliminated the customary JAG review of a military commission's decision.[40]

By far the most shallow, error-ridden account appears in Biddle's memoirs. He wrote that the four Germans at Amagansett had threatened the Coast Guardsman "with revolvers."[41] Nothing in the record supports that claim. Biddle might have been relying on a memo he had written to Roosevelt on June 19, 1942, claiming that one of the four Germans at Amagansett had "covered the Patrolman with a gun."[42] Biddle was in error then and merely repeated it. He said that Dasch "forced $350" into the Guardsman's hand.[43] The figure is either $300 (Dasch's intent) or $260 (what Cullen actually received). Oddly, Biddle's June 19, 1942, memo had it right: $260. According to Biddle, the FBI "was on the job in a few minutes."[44]

37. Cyrus Bernstein, "The Saboteur Trial: A Case History," 11 George Washington Law Review 131, 136 (February 1943).
38. Id. at 157.
39. Id.
40. Id. at 158–59.
41. Biddle, In Brief Authority, at 326.
42. Memo from Biddle to Roosevelt, June 19, 1942, PSF "Departmental File, Justice: Biddle, Francis, 1941–43," Box 56, FDR Library.
43. Biddle, In Brief Authority, at 326.
44. Id.

Eight or so hours would be a better estimate. His description of FBI Director Hoover bordered on hagiography: "All of Edgar Hoover's imaginative and restless energy was stirred into prompt and effective action. His eyes were bright, his jaw set, excitement flickering around the edge of his nostrils when he reported the incident to me."[45] Biddle speculated, with no evidence, that "a particularly brilliant FBI agent, probably attending the school in sabotage where the eight had been trained, had been able to get on the inside."[46] He identified defense counsel Dowell as "McDowell,"[47] and he described an event of July 28, after which he and Royall flew to Philadelphia to urge the Court to call a special session.[48] The trip to Judge Roberts's farm actually took place on July 23. In an error of stunning proportions, Biddle said that *Ex parte Milligan* had been decided "in 1876."[49] An unfortunate typo? Not really. According to Biddle, *Milligan* was issued "a decade after the Civil War."[50] How could a key participant, so close to the record, be so far from it?

Other Evaluations. Alpheus Thomas Mason, in his book on Chief Justice Stone and in an article in a law review, explained Stone's dilemma in drafting an opinion that would do the least damage to the judiciary. The Court could do little other than uphold the jurisdiction of the military tribunal, being "somewhat in the position of a private on sentry duty accosting a commanding general without his pass."[51] Stone was well aware that the judiciary was "in danger of becoming part of an executive juggernaut."[52]

Recent studies of *Quirin* have been quite critical of the Court. To Michal Belknap, Stone went to "such lengths to justify Roosevelt's proclamation" that he preserved the "form" of judicial review while

45. Id. at 327.
46. Id. at 328.
47. Id. at 331.
48. Id. at 337.
49. Id. at 328.
50. Id.
51. Mason, "Inter Arma Silent Leges," at 830.
52. Id. at 831. These views also appear in Alpheus Thomas Mason, Harlan Fiske Stone: Pillar of the Law 665–66 (New York: Viking Press, 1956).

"gutt[ing] it of substance."[53] So long as Justices marched to the beat of war drums, the Court "remained an unreliable guardian of the Bill of Rights."[54] In a separate article, Belknap described Frankfurter in his "Soliloquy" essay as a "judge openly hostile to the accused and manifestly unwilling to afford them procedural safeguards."[55] David J. Danelski called the full opinion in *Quirin* "a rush to judgment, an agonizing effort to justify a *fait accompli*."[56] The opinion represented a victory for the executive branch, but for the Court "an institutional defeat."[57] The lesson for the Court is to "be wary of departing from its established rules and practices, even in times of national crisis, for at such times the Court is especially susceptible to co-optation by the executive."[58]

Saboteur Effort II: 1944–1945

Nazi Germany made a second effort to send saboteurs to the United States by submarine, this time relying on Erich Gimpel, a native of Germany, and William Colepaugh, a Connecticut-born U.S. citizen. Gimpel (age thirty-five) was the more experienced and accomplished of the two. The War Department described Colepaugh (age twenty-six) as "no more than a stooge who, for good reason evidently, was never fully trusted and who was probably never given the true and full details of his and Gimpel's mission."[59] After being trained in sabotage and espionage in schools in Berlin, the Hague, and Dresden, they left Kiel, Germany, on September 26, 1944, on

53. Michal R. Belknap, "The Supreme Court Goes to War: The Meaning and Implications of the Nazi Saboteur Case," 89 Military Law Review 59, 83 (1980).

54. Id. at 95.

55. Michal Belknap, "Frankfurter and the Nazi Saboteurs," Yearbook 1982: Supreme Court Historical Society, at 66.

56. David J. Danelski, "The Saboteurs' Case," 1 Journal of Supreme Court History 61 (1996).

57. Id. at 80.

58. Id.

59. War Department memorandum of January 17, 1945, from Lt. Col. Samuel McKee to Col. Ernest W. Gibson, at 1, RG 319, Records of the Army Staff, Box 275, Gimpel file, National Archives, College Park, Md.

U-boat 1230. It took fifty-four days to cross the Atlantic. On November 29, the sub entered Frenchman's Bay on the coast of Maine, passed between Bar Harbor and Winter Harbor, and proceeded to Hancock Point. There the two men came ashore in a rubber boat.[60]

This time, the FBI had advance notice of German operations. There was evidence that an enemy submarine, traveling westbound in Canadian waters late in November, might enter the Gulf of Maine. The commander of the Eastern Sea Frontier ordered precautionary air sweeps in that area. Beginning November 23, air patrols flew during daylight hours over the water, weather permitting. No contacts were reported.[61] However, when the freighter *Cornwallis* was sunk in Frenchman's Bay on December 3, U.S. authorities suspected that the submarine involved in the attack might have landed saboteurs on the Maine shore.[62] FBI agents traveled to the coastal towns to question residents but learned only that two men, with inadequate clothing, had been seen walking along the road.

Making their way to Bangor, Maine, Gimpel and Colepaugh took a train to Portland and another train to Boston. After one night in Boston they continued on to New York City. Unlike the eight saboteurs in 1942, they brought no explosives with them, although they had received training in the use of thermite and other explosives. Their primary mission: purchase a shortwave radio and transmit intelligence back to Germany. Similar to the 1942 saboteurs, they had been taught to use secret ink to send messages to mail drops in Lisbon and Madrid.[63] Also similar, they bought American clothing, lived well on the U.S. dollars they carried with them, had a falling out, and were picked up by the FBI. Both were apprehended in New York City—Colepaugh on December 26, and Gimpel four days later.

60. "German Agents, Landed by U-Boat, Seized Here by FBI," New York Times, January 2, 1945, at 1.

61. November 1944, War Diary, Chapter II, "Nazi Agents Landed at Hancock, Maine," RG 38, Records of the Office of the Chief of Naval Operations, Eastern Sea Frontier, Box 338, at 1, National Archives, College Park, Md.

62. Id. at 2.

63. "Preliminary Report on the Interrogation of German Saboteurs Erich Gimpel and William C. Colepaugh," at 4, RG 319, Records of the Army Staff, Box 275, Gimpel file, National Archives, College Park, Md.

Colepaugh was taken into custody after meeting with a friend, Edmund F. Mulcahy, who worked as a shoe store clerk in Jamaica, Queens.[64] The two had attended the same private school, the Admiral Farragut Academy. Colepaugh confided to Mulcahy that he was in trouble and had just returned from Germany with someone he feared.[65] Mulcahy contacted the FBI, an agent paid a visit, and soon Colepaugh was divulging all the details. Information from Colepaugh helped FBI agents locate Gimpel.

Initially, it appeared that Gimpel and Colepaugh would be tried in the same manner as the eight Nazi agents in 1942: by a military tribunal sitting on the fifth floor of the Justice Department in Washington, D.C.[66] Biddle was again prepared to conduct the prosecution, along with Cramer. However, Secretary of War Stimson, who thought it had made no sense for Biddle and Cramer to act as prosecutors in 1942, forcefully intervened to block their participation.

Writing to President Roosevelt on January 7, 1945, Stimson cautioned that a repeat of the 1942 procedure "is likely to have unfortunate results." He wanted the trial conducted in the normal manner, "without any extraordinary action or notice taken of the case by officials on the highest levels." He gave several reasons for opposing Biddle's plan. First, a trial of Gimpel and Colepaugh by a military tribunal appointed by the President, with Biddle and Cramer as prosecutors, "would certainly be attended by headlines and worldwide publicity. This would almost certainly lead to charges in Germany that innocent Germans were being tried and condemned by an extraordinary legal proceeding." Second, such a trial "would be likely to lead to German maltreatment of American prisoners of war in their hands." Third, a high-profile military trial would have damaging effects on U.S. fighting troops and the public, because they "would wonder why so much time and such important personnel were devoted to the trial of two obscure persons charged with an ordinary war offense, at a time when millions of Americans are daily risking

64. "Witness Against Spies," New York Times, January 23, 1945, at 21.

65. "Depicts Colepaugh as Fearing Gimpel," New York Times, February 9, 1945, at 9.

66. "Army to Try Spies, Roosevelt Hints," New York Times, January 3, 1945, at 1; "Boy Hero Arrives," New York Times, January 4, 1945, at 21.

their lives." For these reasons, Stimson advised that the men should be tried by either court-martial or military commission, with the appointment authority placed in the Army Commander in Boston or New York.[67]

With Biddle generating support for his appointment as prosecutor, Stimson took care to develop his own list of backers. His prediction of what the Germans would do to American POWs, he told Roosevelt, came from "high military authorities." Moreover, he informed Roosevelt that Elmer Davis of the Office of War Information concurred in these views "regarding the public relation aspect and also as to the use that the Germans would make of the case."[68] Biddle insisted that Roosevelt appoint the commission,[69] whereas Stimson wanted the appointment power lodged in "the appropriate Army commander."[70]

In his diary, Stimson expressed contempt for Biddle's grandstanding. At a Cabinet meeting, Stimson told Roosevelt that he "wouldn't favor any high-ranking officers as members of the tribunal and did not propose to have the Judge Advocate General personally try it." If Biddle appeared in person at a trial held in Washington, "it would inevitably turn it into a dramatic performance which would be played up by the press." Stimson, indicating that Roosevelt apparently agreed with him "fully," noted that Biddle continued to press his position. After returning from the meeting, Stimson spoke to a colleague in the War Department about Biddle's attitude: "It is a petty thing. That little man is such a small little man and so anxious for publicity that he is trying to make an enormous show out of this performance—the trial of two miserable spies. The President was all on my side but he may be pulled over."[71]

Biddle wrote to Stimson on January 8, spelling out his objections

67. Letter from Stimson to Roosevelt, January 7, 1945, at 1–2, RG 107, Records of the Office of the Secretary of War, Stimson's "Safe File," National Archives, College Park, Md. (hereafter Stimson's Safe File).

68. Id.

69. Letter from Biddle to Stimson, January 8, 1945, Stimson's Safe File.

70. Letter from Stimson to Biddle, January 8, 1945, id.

71. Stimson Diary, January 5, 1945, at 18–19.

to trial by a court-martial appointed by the commanding officer of
the military district where the two men had landed. He believed that
in a court-martial the defense counsel would complicate the case by
citing procedural protections in the Articles of War and the *Manual
for Courts-Martial.* The *Manual,* he noted, provided that an accused "cannot be convicted legally upon his unsupported confession." Without the confessions from Colepaugh and Gimpel, Biddle
doubted that a court-martial could convict them. Biddle also objected that a court-martial would require that the trial record go first
to a board of review and then to the Judge Advocate General, instead of directly to the President, as in 1942. He continued to insist
that Roosevelt appoint the military commission and that the prosecution be conducted jointly by the Justice Department and the
Judge Advocate General.[72] On the same day, Biddle transmitted
those positions to Roosevelt.[73]

In a diary entry for January 8, Stimson seemed a little more con-
fident that he would prevail. He said that two of Roosevelt's aides,
Judge Sam Rosenman and Press Secretary Steve Early, were on his
side.[74] Early sent a memo to Rosenman on January 8, backing Stimson.[75] On the following day, a Rosenman memo told Early that
James Byrnes should be brought in to settle the interdepartmental
dispute.[76] On January 10, Roosevelt asked Byrnes to look into the
matter, indicating that he felt "rather strongly" that the trial should
be handled by Stimson, with some help from the Justice Department, and that the trial should be conducted on Governors Island
"with the least amount of publicity."[77] As director of the Office of
War Mobilization and Reconversion, Byrnes replied to Roosevelt
that the two saboteurs should be tried by court-martial or military
commission, appointed by the Army commander. He discounted

72. Letter from Biddle to Stimson, January 8, 1945, "Confidential File, War Department, 1944–45," PSF, Box 10, FDR Library.
73. Letter from Biddle to Roosevelt, January 8, 1945, id.
74. Stimson Diary, January 8, 1945, at 23.
75. Memo from Early to Rosenman, January 8, 1945, "Confidential File, War Department, 1944–45," PSF, Box 10, FDR Library.
76. Memo from Rosenman to Early, January 9, 1945, id.
77. Memo from Roosevelt to Byrnes, January 10, 1945, id.

Biddle's argument that legal technicalities might complicate a conviction. Byrnes favored leaving the matter to the War Department.[78]

Stimson won the battle. On January 12, Roosevelt released a military order to try Gimpel and Colepaugh. Unlike in his military order of July 2, 1942, he did not name the members of the tribunal or the counsel for the prosecution and defense. Instead, he empowered the commanding generals, under the supervision of the Secretary of War, "to appoint military commissions for the trial of such persons." Moreover, the trial record would not go directly to the President, as it had in 1942. The review would be processed within the Judge Advocate General's office: "The record of the trial, including any judgment or sentence, shall be promptly reviewed under the procedures established in Article 50½ of the Articles of War."[79]

Appointments to the seven-man tribunal were made by Maj. Gen. Thomas A. Terry, commander of the Second Service Command. He also selected the officers to serve as prosecutors and defense counsel. In addition to the military personnel, two members from the Justice Department assisted with the prosecution.[80] Biddle had no role as prosecutor, and Cramer's participation was limited to his review function within the JAG office. The trial took place not in Washington, D.C., but at Governors Island, New York City.[81] Unlike the 1942 military trial, much of the testimony leaked to the press.[82]

On February 14, 1945, the tribunal sentenced Colepaugh and Gimpel to death by hanging. They had been found guilty of three counts: violation of the law of war by passing through military lines, violation of the 82nd Article of War for spying, and conspiracy. The tribunal deliberated for three hours. The verdicts and sentences went

78. Memo from Byrnes to Roosevelt, January 11, 1945, id.

79. Military Order, 10 Fed. Reg. 548 (1945).

80. "2 Spy Suspects Given to Army for Trial," New York Times, January 19, 1945, at 14.

81. "Spy Trials Open Today," New York Times, February 6, 1945, at 5.

82. "Spy Suspects Had 2-Year Task Here," New York Times, February 10, 1945, at 7; "Spy Relates How He Joined Nazis," New York Times, February 11, 1945, at 8; "Spy Suspect Cites 'Disillusionment,'" New York Times, February 13, 1945, at 10; "Testimony Closes at Trial Here," New York Times, February 14, 1945, at 4.

to General Terry, as the appointing officer, and from there to the Judge Advocate General's office.[83]

President Roosevelt died on April 12, before the executions could be carried out. On May 8, President Harry Truman announced the end of the war in Europe. The following month, he commuted the death sentences of the two men to life imprisonment.[84] In 1955, the U.S. government released Gimpel from prison and deported him to Germany.[85] Colepaugh, without success, initiated a habeas corpus action from prison, arguing that he should not have been tried by a military tribunal.[86] He was paroled in 1960.[87]

(unclear) Thus, the Administration had learned several lessons from the 1942 experience. Military tribunals should not be spectacular show trials in the nation's capital, the prosecution should not be conducted by the Attorney General and the Judge Advocate General, the President should not be the appointing official, and he should not receive the trial record directly from the tribunal. Instead, review of the trial record should be performed by trained and experienced experts within the Office of the Judge Advocate General.

World War II Trials

Throughout the war years, federal courts largely deferred to executive and military authorities. Traditional constitutional rights, including the writ of habeas corpus, were set aside in some communities. Only after the war did the judiciary begin to recapture lost territory and defend citizen rights against military rule. Courts began to place restrictions on both military tribunals and courts-martial.

83. "2 Spies Sentenced to Die by Hanging," New York Times, February 15, 1945, at 1.
84. "Truman Commutes to Life Terms Death Sentences of Two Spies," New York Times, June 24, 1945, at 1.
85. "'44 Nazi Spy Landed in U-boat Is Deported to West Germany," New York Times, August 13, 1955, at 15.
86. Colepaugh v. Looney, 235 F.2d 429 (10th Cir. 1956), cert. denied, 352 U.S. 1014 (1957).
87. "An American Was the Nazi Spy Next Door," USA Today, February 28, 2002, at 2A.

- Provost courts; fine pay fine
- Military Commission, death penalty
RETHINKING TRIBUNALS   145

Even before the United States entered World War II, the Supreme Court gave an inkling of how individual rights can be subordinated to what government considers the higher priority of national security. In 1940, the Court upheld a compulsory flag salute against the claims of Jehovah's Witnesses that the salute violated their religious beliefs. Writing for an eight-to-one majority, Justice Frankfurter leaned heavily on two premises: liberty requires unifying sentiments, and national unity promotes national security.[88]

The *New Republic,* which Frankfurter had helped found, warned that the country was "in great danger of adopting Hitler's philosophy in the effort to oppose Hitler's legions." It accused the Court of coming "dangerously close to being a victim of [war] hysteria."[89] Mark DeWolfe Howe called the decision "a disheartening omen of the Court's unwillingness when chauvinism is loose in the land to safeguard the dissenter."[90] The Court reversed itself in 1943, but credit for the liberalized decision belongs to those who opposed the Court's position on minority rights and religious liberty and built pressure for the eventual turnabout.[91]

Martial Law in Hawaii. After the December 7, 1941, attack on Pearl Harbor, Governor J. B. Poindexter issued a proclamation at 3:30 that afternoon, turning over all governmental functions (including judicial) to Lt. Gen. Walter C. Short, Commanding General of the Hawaiian Department. On that same day, Short assumed the role of "Military Governor." He ordered the courts to close and replaced them with two forms of military tribunal: provost courts, authorized to impose fines up to $5,000 and imprisonment of up to five years, and a Military Commission, which could impose more severe sentences, including the death penalty.

88. Minersville School District v. Gobitis, 310 U.S. 586 (1940).
89. "Frankfurter v. Stone," New Republic, June 24, 1940, at 843, 844.
90. Mark DeWolfe Howe, The Garden and the Wilderness: Religion and Government in American Constitutional History 111 (Chicago: University of Chicago Press, 1965).
91. West Virginia State Board of Education v. Barnette, 319 U.S. 624 (1943). See also Louis Fisher, Religious Liberty in America: Political Safeguards 105–14 (Lawrence: University Press of Kansas, 2002).

On December 14, 1942, the Ninth Circuit upheld the authority of the Governor of Hawaii to suspend until further notice the privilege of the writ of habeas corpus.[92] Although no charges had been filed against the defendant, Hans Zimmerman, the military kept him in prison. He was held under general suspicion of subversive and disloyal activities. The Ninth Circuit said that civil courts "are ill adapted to cope with an emergency of this kind. As a rule they proceed only upon formal charges."[93] In a dissent, Judge Haney said that the government had admitted during oral argument that there were no charges against Zimmerman for violating the U.S. Constitution, a federal statute, a statute of the Territory of Hawaii, the Articles of War, the law of war, or any order of the President, the Secretary of War, the Military Governor, or any other commanding officer.[94] Later, the Supreme Court denied certiorari on the ground that the case was moot, "it appearing that Hans Zimmerman . . . has been released from the respondent's custody."[95]

Although the federal courts acquiesced in this case, District Judge Delbert E. Metzger confronted the military's detention of two other men in Hawaii, Walter Glockner and Erwin R. Seifer. In July 1943, Metzger issued a writ of habeas corpus to have the two men produced in court. When the military refused, he fined Lt. Gen. Robert C. Richardson, Jr., Commander of the Hawaiian Department, $5,000 for contempt. Richardson upped the ante by ordering Metzger to purge the court's records of the contempt proceedings and threatened to punish Metzger through either the provost courts or the Military Commission. The Justice Department rushed in to have that order rescinded and asked Metzger to expunge the contempt judgment and remit the fine. He declined to do that, but he did reduce the fine to $100, which President Roosevelt later canceled through a pardon.[96]

92. Ex parte Zimmerman, 132 F.2d 442 (9th Cir. 1942).

93. Id. at 446.

94. Id. at 452.

95. Zimmerman v. Walker, 319 U.S. 744 (1943).

96. Claude McColloch, "Now It Can Be Told: Judge Metzger and the Military," 35 American Bar Association Journal 365 (1949).

Other cases of military arrest in Hawaii came forward. Fred Spurlock, a black American, was brought before a provost court and charged with assaulting a civilian policeman. He was placed on probation, but after he got into trouble again, the provost court sentenced him to five years at hard labor. A federal district court held that the provost court lacked jurisdiction over either Spurlock or the charge brought against him, and that its judgment of conviction was thus null and void.[97] The Ninth Circuit reversed the district court.[98] After other Hawaiian martial law cases had been accepted by the Supreme Court, General Richardson intervened to grant Spurlock a pardon.[99]

Japanese-Americans. The greatest wartime deprivation of individual rights in the United States involved the Japanese-Americans. In 1943, the Court unanimously upheld a curfew order directed against more than 100,000 Japanese-Americans, about two-thirds of them natural-born U.S. citizens.[100] The curfew had been supported by Executive Order 9066, promulgated by President Roosevelt on February 19, 1942, and by legislation enacted by Congress on March 21, 1942. A concurrence by Justice Douglas said, "we cannot sit in judgment on the military requirements of that hour."[101]

A concurrence by Justice Murphy was more critical of the ruling. He said that the "broad guaranties of the Bill of Rights and other provisions of the Constitution protecting essential liberties" are not suspended by the "mere existence of a state of war." The Court should never forget that "there are constitutional boundaries which it is our duty to uphold." Singling out the Japanese-American population disturbed him: "Distinctions based on color and ancestry are utterly inconsistent with our traditions and ideals. They are at variance with the principles for which we are now waging war."[102] The

97. Ex parte Spurlock, 66 F.Supp. 997, 1003 (D. Haw. 1944).
98. Steer v. Spurlock, 146 F.2d 652 (9th Cir. 1944).
99. 92 Cong. Rec. A4673 (1946).
100. Hirabayashi v. United States, 320 U.S. 81 (1943).
101. Id. at 106.
102. Id. at 110.

curfew policy toward the Japanese-Americans, he said, "bears a melancholy resemblance to the treatment accorded to members of the Jewish race in Germany and in other parts of Europe."[103] Then came this blunt warning: "In my opinion this goes to the very brink of constitutional power."[104] A third concurrence by Justice Rutledge also indicated that he might not tolerate heavier sanctions against the Japanese-Americans. A military officer required wide discretion, but "it does not follow there may not be bounds beyond which he cannot go and, if he oversteps them, that the courts may not have power to protect the civilian citizen."[105]

A year later, the Court split six to three in upholding the placement of Japanese-Americans in detention camps.[106] In the first of the dissents, Justice Roberts distinguished this case from the previous one "of keeping people off the streets at night."[107] Instead, it was a case of "convicting a citizen as a punishment for not submitting to imprisonment in a concentration camp, based on his ancestry, and solely because of his ancestry, without evidence or inquiry concerning his loyalty and good disposition towards the United States."[108] In language unusually blunt for a Justice, he called Assembly Centers a "euphemism for a prison" and Relocation Centers "a euphemism for concentration camps."[109]

True to his warning, Justice Murphy said that the exclusion of Japanese-Americans "goes over 'the brink of constitutional power' and falls into the ugly abyss of racism."[110] In this dissent, he did not deny that there were disloyal persons of Japanese descent on the Pacific Coast, but the same could be said of Germans and Italians.[111] He insisted that under the American system of law, individual guilt—not group guilt—"is the sole basis for deprivation of

103. Id. at 111.
104. Id.
105. Id. at 114.
106. Korematsu v. United States, 323 U.S. 214 (1944).
107. Id. at 225.
108. Id. at 226.
109. Id. at 230.
110. Id. at 233.
111. Id. at 240.

rights."[112] He pointed out that "not one person of Japanese ancestry was accused or convicted of espionage or sabotage after Pearl Harbor while they were still free."[113] In a stunning repudiation of the decision, he called it a "legalization of racism."[114] This ruling convinced Murphy that it was time to impose judicial checks on the growth of military power.[115]

In a third dissent, Justice Jackson reminded the Court that "if any fundamental assumption underlies our system, it is that guilt is personal and not inheritable."[116] Article III of the Constitution, he said, specifically forbade punishment because of treasonable acts by parents or ancestors: "no Attainder of Treason shall work Corruption of Blood, or Forfeiture except during the Life of the Person attainted." Yet here was an attempt by the government "to make an otherwise innocent act a crime merely because this prisoner is the son of parents as to whom he had no choice, and belongs to a race from which there is no way to resign."[117] He warned of the dangers when the Court lent its endorsement to military orders:

A military order, however unconstitutional, is not apt to last longer than the military emergency. Even during that period a succeeding commander may revoke it all. But once a judicial opinion rationalizes such an order to show that it conforms to the Constitution, or rather rationalizes the Constitution to show that the Constitution sanctions such an order, the Court for all time has validated the principle of racial discrimination in criminal procedure and of transplanting American citizens. The principle then lies about like a loaded weapon ready for the hand of any authority that can bring forward a plausible claim of an urgent need.[118]

In later years, Jackson wrote more searchingly about the kinds of judicial weaknesses and vulnerabilities that can result in the loss of

112. Id.
113. Id. at 241.
114. Id. at 242.
115. J. Woodford Howard, Jr., Mr. Justice Murphy: A Political Biography 367 (Princeton, N.J.: Princeton University Press, 1968).
116. 323 U.S. at 243.
117. Id.
118. 323 U.S. at 246.

individual freedoms and constitutional rights. The Court "can never quite escape consciousness of its own infirmities, a psychology which may explain its apparent yielding to expediency, especially during war time."[119]

Earl Warren was Attorney General of California during the war years and supported these actions against the Japanese-Americans. Once on the Court, as Chief Justice, he regretted the nation's actions and particularly the record of the judiciary. In a law review article in 1962, he made a remarkable statement that decisions in the Japanese-American cases "that a given program is constitutional, does not necessarily answer the question whether, in a broader sense, it actually is."[120] No one has ever more effectively shot holes in the claim that the Court has a monopoly (or wisdom) in interpreting the Constitution. The Court's failure to invalidate the government's actions against the Japanese-Americans did not mean that constitutional standards had been followed. Far from it. In a democratic society, Warren said, "it is still the Legislature and the elected Executive who have the primary responsibility for fashioning and executing policy consistent with the Constitution."[121]

The Yamashita Case. After dividing on the Japanese-American cases, the Court split again on the military trial of Gen. Tomoyuki Yamashita. As Commanding General of the Japanese Fourteenth Army Group in the Philippine Islands, he was charged by a military commission with failing to control the operations of his troops, allowing them to commit specified atrocities against the civilian population and prisoners of war. The commission consisted of five American generals, none of them lawyers.[122] Moreover, none of the

119. Robert H. Jackson, The Supreme Court in the American System of Government 25 (Cambridge: Harvard University Press, 1955).

120. Earl Warren, "The Bill of Rights and the Military," 37 New York University Law Review 181, 193 (1962).

121. Id. at 202.

122. J. Gordon Feldhaus, "The Trial of Yamashita," 15 South Dakota Bar Journal 181, 185 (October 1946).

generals had any serious combat command experience.[123] Yamashita filed a petition for a writ of habeas corpus to the Court, contending that the commission was without lawful authority or jurisdiction to place him on trial. The Court pointed to "congressional recognition of military commissions and its sanction of their use in trying offenses against the law of war."[124]

A dissent by Justice Murphy agreed that the commission had been authorized by the power of Congress to "define and punish . . . Offences against the Law of Nations," but he charged that Yamashita's rights under the Due Process Clause of the Fifth Amendment "were grossly and openly violated without any justification."[125] He had been "rushed to trial under an improper charge, given insufficient time to prepare an adequate defense, deprived of the benefits of some of the most elementary rules of evidence and summarily sentenced to be hanged."[126] Although "brutal atrocities" had been inflicted upon the Filipino population by Japanese armed forces under Yamashita's command,[127] there was no evidence that he knew of the atrocities or in any way ordered them. In fact, U.S. forces had done everything possible to disrupt his control over Japanese troops. Murphy objected that to "use the very inefficiency and disorganization created by the victorious forces as the primary basis for condemning officers of the defeated armies bears no resemblance to justice or to military reality."[128]

In a separate dissent, Justice Rutledge concluded that the proceedings and rules of evidence of the Yamashita commission had violated two Articles of War enacted by Congress.[129] It was not in the American tradition "to be charged with crime which is defined

123. Stephen B. Ives, Jr., "Vengeance Did Not Deliver Justice," Washington Post, December 30, 2001, at B2.
124. In re Yamashita, 327 U.S. 1, 10 (1946).
125. Id. at 26, 40.
126. Id. at 27–28.
127. Id. at 29.
128. Id. at 35.
129. Id. at 61

after his conduct, alleged to be criminal, has taken place; or in language not sufficient to inform him of the nature of the offense or to enable him to make defense."[130] Although *Ex parte Quirin* ruled that the Court had no authority to review the evidence before a military commission, "it was not there or elsewhere determined that it could not ascertain whether conviction is founded upon evidence expressly excluded by Congress or treaty; nor does the Court purport to do so now."[131] Rutledge devoted one section of his dissent to explain how Articles of War 25 and 38 deprived the military commission of jurisdiction to try or punish General Yamashita,[132] while a separate section concluded that Yamashita's trial was in conflict with the Geneva Convention of 1929.[133]

For those present at the trial, it was evident that "many of the troops that had committed the atrocities alleged in the bill of particulars were not at the time under Yamashita's command, but under the command of the 4th Air Army Headquarters or Maritime Transport Command."[134] Yamashita, known as "The Tiger of Malaya" for defeating the British at Singapore, did not reach the Philippines until October 7, 1944, and had nothing to do with the death march from Manila to Carbannatuan.[135]

A Revival of Milligan?

By 1945, the Supreme Court was prepared to place limits on martial law in Hawaii. One case involved Lloyd Duncan, a civilian shipfitter

---

130. Id. at 43.

131. Id. at 47.

132. Id. at 61–72.

133. Id. at 72–78. Murphy and Rutledge also issued dissenting opinions when the Court denied leave to file petition for a writ of habeas corpus in another military tribunal case of a Japanese general; Homma v. Patterson, 327 U.S. 759 (1946).

134. Feldhaus, "The Trial of Yamashita," at 188. Feldhaus was part of Yamashita's defense team; id. at 185.

135. Id. at 183. For details of the trial by another member of the defense team, see A. Frank Reel, The Case of General Yamashita (Chicago: University of Chicago Press, 1949).

employed in the Navy Yard at Honolulu. He was tried and sentenced to imprisonment by a provost court for assaulting two Marine sentries on duty at the Navy Yard. By the time the case reached Judge Metzger, Governor Ingram M. Stainback (who succeeded Governor Poindexter) had issued a proclamation on February 8, 1943, restoring within thirty days some powers and functions to civilian agencies, including civil and criminal courts.[136] Moreover, after the decisive U.S. defeat of the Japanese Navy at Midway in June 1942, both General Richardson and Adm. Chester Nimitz agreed that a Japanese invasion of Hawaii was now practically impossible.[137] Judge Metzger held that the Organic Act of Hawaii gave Governor Poindexter no power to transfer or abdicate his authority to military officials[138] and that martial law did not lawfully exist in Hawaii in 1943, particularly after March 10, 1943 (the effective date of Governor Stainback's proclamation).[139] Therefore, the office of Military Governor possessed no lawful authority over civilian affairs or persons, and the provost court lacked authority to try, find guilty, or sentence civilians.[140] A similar decision was handed down by another district court.[141]

The Ninth Circuit reversed both decisions,[142] but on February 12, 1945, the Supreme Court granted certiorari to hear the two cases.[143] The Court held that the armed forces in Hawaii lacked the authority, during a period of martial law, to supplant all civilian laws and to substitute military tribunals for judicial trials of civilians not charged with violations of the law of war. The case was decided not on the scope of presidential power but on what Congress had intended when it enacted the Organic Act of Hawaii.[144] The Court held that although Congress anticipated that the Governor of Hawaii,

136. Ex parte Duncan, 66 F.Supp. 976, 979 (D. Haw. 1944).
137. Id.
138. Id. at 981.
139. Id.
140. Id. at 981–82.
141. Ex parte White, 66 F.Supp. 982 (D. Haw. 1944).
142. Ex parte Duncan, 146 F.2d 576 (9th Cir. 1944).
143. Duncan v. Kahanamoku, & White v. Steer, 324 U.S. 833 (1945).
144. Duncan v. Kahanamoku, 327 U.S. 304 (1946).

with the approval of the President, could invoke military aid under certain circumstances, it did not explicitly declare that the Governor acting with the military could use military tribunals to close all the civil courts "for days, months or years."[145]

In 1948, the Court declined to review a military tribunal created in Japan by Gen. Douglas MacArthur. Relying on a legal fiction that the tribunal acted as the agent of the Allied Powers, rather than of the United States, it held that U.S. courts had no power or authority to review, affirm, set aside, or annul the judgments and sentences imposed by the tribunal on the residents and citizens of Japan.[146] A concurrence by Justice Douglas expressed uneasiness with the decision: "if no United States court can inquire into the lawfulness of [an individual's] detention, the military have acquired, contrary to our traditions (see *Ex parte Quirin,* 317 U.S. 1; *In re Yamashita,* 327 U.S. 1), a new and alarming hold on us."[147]

Two years later, the Court received another case testing the scope of military commissions. The issue was whether nonresident enemy aliens, tried and convicted in China by an American military commission for violations of the laws of war committed in China, had a right to a writ of habeas corpus to U.S. civilian courts. Similar to the situation of martial law in Hawaii, a lower federal court was willing to place limits on the military, but the Supreme Court was not. The D.C. Circuit held that any person deprived of liberty by U.S. officials is entitled to show that his confinement violates the Constitution, regardless of whether he is a citizen or an alien. The appellate court noted that the Fifth Amendment applies broadly to "any person."[148] The court denied that its decision created a practical problem of transporting the twenty-one appellants to the United States for a hearing, pointing out that the Supreme Court had decided *Quirin* without the personal presence of the German saboteurs.[149]

145. Id. at 315.
146. Hirota v. MacArthur, 338 U.S. 197 (1948).
147. Id. at 201–2.
148. Eisentrager v. Forrestal, 174 F.2d 961, 963 (D.C. Cir. 1949).
149. Id. at 968.

The Supreme Court reversed. Unlike the eight Germans in *Quirin,* these prisoners had never been or lived in the United States, were captured outside U.S. territory, were tried and convicted by a military commission sitting outside the United States for offenses against laws of war committed outside the United States, and were at all times imprisoned outside the United States.[150] In denying the writ of habeas corpus and refusing review for these petitioners, the Court looked less to the power of Congress and the President than to the meaning of "any person" in the Fifth Amendment. It noted that if the Fifth Amendment "invests enemy aliens in unlawful hostile action against us with immunity from military trial, it puts them in a more protected position than our own soldiers. . . . It would be a paradox indeed if what the Amendment denied to Americans it guaranteed to enemies."[151] Writing for the Court, Justice Jackson said that it was "not for us to say whether these prisoners were or were not guilty of a war crime, or whether if we were to retry the case we would agree to the findings of fact or the application of the laws of war made by the Military Commission."[152]

In deciding these cases, the Court seemed to exclude judicial review of military tribunals if they were located outside the country. A dissent by Justices Black, Douglas, and Burton accused the Court of fashioning a "wholly indefensible" doctrine by permitting the executive branch, "by deciding where its prisoners will be tried and imprisoned, to deprive all federal courts of their power to protect against a federal executive's illegal incarceration."[153] To say that petitioners were denied the privilege of habeas corpus "solely because they were convicted and imprisoned overseas" was to adopt "a broad and dangerous principle."[154] The government's brief had argued that habeas corpus was not available even to U.S. citizens convicted and imprisoned in Germany by American military tribunals.[155]

150. Johnson v. Eisentrager, 339 U.S. 763, 777 (1950).
151. Id. at 783.
152. Id. at 786.
153. Id. at 795.
154. Id.
155. Id.

That precise issue reached the Court in 1952. Yvette Madsen, a native-born U.S. citizen, was charged with murdering her husband, an officer of the U.S. Air Force. She was convicted in Germany by a military commission consisting of three U.S. citizens, with review by a military appellate court of five U.S. citizens. In upholding the actions of these military commissions, the Court examined the relative powers of the President and Congress. It concluded that the President, in the "absence of attempts by Congress to limit the President's power," may in time of war "establish and prescribe the jurisdiction and procedure of military commissions."[156] It further noted: "The policy of Congress to refrain from legislating in this uncharted area does not imply its lack of power to legislate."[157] Black penned the sole dissent, insisting that if American citizens in Germany are to be tried by the American government, "they should be tried under laws passed by Congress and in courts created by Congress under its constitutional authority."[158]

The broad scope given to military trials did not begin to narrow until 1955. In that year, the Court reviewed the court-martial of an ex-serviceman after he had served in Korea, been honorably discharged, and returned to the United States. Initially the Justices lined up behind the military, but Black led the dissenters to insist that the case be reargued, particularly after the confirmation of John Harlan as Associate Justice. After scheduling the rehearing, Chief Justice Earl Warren announced at conference that he had changed his position, shifting the majority to Black.[159]

Writing for the Court, Black invoked Article III and the Bill of Rights to place restrictions on what Congress could do under its Article I powers and what a President may do as Commander in Chief in asserting military authority over citizens. The Court ruled that ex-servicemen must be tried in federal civil courts.[160] Although the

156. Madsen v. Kinsella, 343 U.S. 341, 348 (1952).
157. Id. at 348–49.
158. Id. at 372.
159. Bernard Schwartz, Super Chief 180–81 (New York: New York University Press, 1983).
160. Toth v. Quarles, 350 U.S. 11 (1955).

case focused on a court-martial, its reasoning could apply to military tribunals: "We find nothing in the history or constitutional treatment of military tribunals which entitles them to rank along with Article III courts as adjudicators of the guilt or innocence of people charged with offenses for which they can be deprived of their life, liberty or property."[161]

A series of cases from 1956 to 1960 reviewed the constitutionality of using courts-martial to try civilian dependents of military personnel living overseas. In one case, the wife of an Army colonel was tried by a general court-martial in Tokyo for murdering her husband. After she was found guilty and sentenced to life imprisonment, the Court found no constitutional deficiency in the proceeding.[162] This decision came down on June 11, 1956, just as the Court was wrapping up its business for the term. In a "Reservation," Frankfurter delicately referred to some hasty actions: "Doubtless because of the pressure under which the Court works during its closing weeks," several arguments "have been merely adumbrated in its opinion."[163] That was fancy language for saying that the Court had given inadequate time and attention to the case. A dissent by Warren, Black, and Douglas was more blunt: "The questions raised are complex, the remedy drastic, and the consequences far-reaching upon the lives of civilians. The military is given new powers not hitherto thought consistent with our scheme of government. For these reasons, we need more time than is available in these closing days of the Term in which to write our dissenting views. We will file our dissents during the next Term of Court."[164]

On that same day, the Court held that Clarice Covert could be convicted and sentenced to life imprisonment by a court-martial in England for the murder of her husband, an Air Force sergeant. She was brought to the United States and confined in the Federal Reformatory for Women in Alderson, West Virginia. The Court distinguished this

161. Id. at 17.
162. Kinsella v. Krueger, 351 U.S. 470 (1956).
163. Id. at 483.
164. Id. at 485–86.

case from _Toth_ v. _Quarles,_ involving the serviceman who had been honorably discharged.[165] The dissent by Warren, Black, and Douglas applied to the Covert case as well.

The unseemly haste in cranking out decisions at the last minute prompted the dissenters to pressure the Court to rehear the "Cases of the Murdering Wives."[166] After granting a petition for rehearing, the Court reversed both decisions and ruled that when the United States acts against its citizens abroad, it must act in accordance with all the limitations imposed by the Constitution, including Article III and the Fifth and Sixth Amendments. Such citizens must be tried in Article III courts.[167] The reasoning was broad enough to cover not only courts-martial but also military tribunals. Dependents of military personnel overseas "could not constitutionally be tried by military authorities."[168]

While acknowledging that "it has not yet been definitively established to what extent the President, as Commander-in-Chief of the armed forces," can promulgate the procedures of military courts in time of peace or war, and conceding that Congress "has given the President broad discretion to provide the rules governing military trials," the Court issued this cautionary note:

If the President can provide rules of substantive law as well as procedure, then he and his military subordinates exercise legislative, executive and judicial powers with respect to those subject to military trials. Such blending of functions in one branch of the Government is the objectionable thing which the draftsmen of the Constitution endeavored to prevent by providing for the separation of governmental powers.[169]

Other decisions during this period placed restrictions on the use of courts-martial abroad to try civilian dependents of military personnel and civilian employees of the armed forces.[170]

165. Reid v. Covert, 351 U.S. 487, 491 (1956).
166. Schwartz, Super Chief, at 239–43.
167. Reid v. Covert, 354 U.S. 1 (1957).
168. Id. at 5.
169. Id. at 38–39.
170. Kinsella v. Singleton, 361 U.S. 234 (1960); McElroy v. Guagliardo, 361 U.S. 281 (1960); Grisham v. Hagan, 361 U.S. 278 (1960).

followed the same rule as Roosevelt

Bush's Military Order in 2001

By 2001, the issue of military tribunals seemed quaint if not anti-quated. Few people could recall *Ex parte Quirin* or what had happened to the eight German saboteurs. All that changed rapidly on November 13, 2001, when President George W. Bush issued a military order authorizing a military commission to try those who had provided assistance for the terrorist attacks of September 11 in New York City and Washington, D.C. In many respects, the Bush order tracked the Roosevelt proclamation and military order of 1942. Conviction and sentencing would require the vote of only two-thirds of the members of the commission, the same fraction used in the Roosevelt order. Bush's tribunal could admit evidence that would have "probative value to a reasonable person." The Roosevelt order spoke of "probative value to a reasonable man." Bush directed the Secretary of Defense to develop orders and regulations for the conduct of the proceedings and other matters.

Roosevelt cautioned his military tribunal to conduct a "full and fair trial." Bush used the identical phrase. Also, Bush adopted Roosevelt's prohibition against judicial review. A defendant "shall not be privileged to seek any remedy or maintain any proceeding, directly or indirectly, or to have any such remedy or proceeding sought on the individual's behalf in (i) any court of the United States, or any State thereof, (ii) any court of any foreign nation, or (iii) any international tribunal."[171] Roosevelt's order denied access to civil courts, except under such regulations as the Attorney General, with the approval of the Secretary of War, may prescribe.[172] That exception did not appear in the Bush order.

The Bush order directed that the trial record, including any conviction or sentence, be submitted for review and final decision "by

171. 66 Fed. Reg. 57835–36, sec. 7.
172. 7 Fed. Reg. 5101 (1942). The second military order by President Roosevelt on January 12, 1945, did not prohibit judicial review (10 Fed. Reg. 549). It is not clear whether this second order stands alone or must be read in concert with the 1942 procla-mation. In 1956, the Tenth Circuit assumed the latter. Colepaugh v. Looney, 235 F.2d 429, 431 (10th Cir. 1956).

Different b/w FDR & Bush

160   NAZI SABOTEURS ON TRIAL

me or by the Secretary of Defense if so designated by me for that
purpose." The Roosevelt order of 1942 directed that the trial record,
including any judgment or sentence, be transmitted directly to him
for action. The Bush order did not follow the Roosevelt order of
1945, which processed the review first through the office of the
Judge Advocate General, although nothing prevented the Administration from adopting that procedure.

There are some marked differences between the Bush order and
the Roosevelt precedents. The latter applied to eight saboteurs in
1942 and two in 1945. Bush's order covered a much larger population: any individual "not a United States citizen" that the President
determines there is "reason to believe" (i) "is or was a member of the
organization known as al Qaida," (ii) "has engaged in, aided or abet-
ted, or conspired to commit, acts of international terrorism, or acts
in preparation therefor, that have caused, threaten to cause, or have
as their aim to cause, injury to or adverse effects on the United
States, its citizens, national security, foreign policy, or economy," or
(iii) has "knowingly harbored one or more individuals described in
subparagraph (i) and (ii)."

By restricting the order to non-U.S. citizens, Bush seemed to respect the principle in *Milligan* that U.S. citizens are entitled to be
tried in civil courts when they are open and functioning. Yet his
group of noncitizens and resident aliens represented a population of
an estimated 18 million people. FDR had looked backward at a
handful of known saboteurs who had confessed. Bush looked forward to a large population of unknowns, not yet apprehended or
charged. The portion of non-U.S. citizens at risk depended on presidential "determinations" and the definitions of such phrases as "international terrorism," "have as their aim," and "knowingly harbor."
"Aiding or abetting" could involve innocently contributing money
to a group that seemed to be a legitimate charitable or humanitarian
organization but in fact operated as a front by providing assistance
to al Qaeda or other terrorist bodies.

Administration's Defense. Vice President Dick Cheney supported
Bush's military order by arguing that terrorists, because they are not

lawful combatants, "don't deserve to be treated as a prisoner of war." He spoke favorably of the treatment of the German saboteurs in 1942, who had been "executed in relatively rapid order."[173] The concept of a military tribunal had been developed by William P. Barr, former Attorney General in the first Bush Administration. Barr's previous position with the Justice Department, as head of the Office of Legal Counsel (OLC), put him in the same space occupied by the 1942 military tribunal. He said that the idea of a tribunal had come to him as one way to try the men charged with blowing up the Pan Am jetliner over Lockerbie, Scotland.[174] In an op-ed piece with Andrew G. McBride, Barr referred to the case of the eight Nazi saboteurs as the "most apt precedent."[175]

Although the Administration lined up behind the proposal, one official told a reporter that it was "unlikely" that the tribunals would operate on U.S. territory.[176] That position seemed underscored when Attorney General John Ashcroft defended military tribunals in this manner: "Foreign terrorists who commit war crimes against the United States, in my judgment, are not entitled to and do not deserve the protection of the American Constitution, particularly when there could be very serious and important reasons related to not bringing them back to the United States for justice."[177] To Ashcroft, the issue seemed clear: if you are a foreign terrorist, you do not deserve constitutional rights. The key legal issue, of course, is demonstrating that someone *is* a foreign terrorist. Reaching that judgment requires the fact-finding and procedural protections of an independent court capable of distinguishing between the guilty and the innocent. Ashcroft seemed to assume guilt in advance.

173. "Senior Administration Officials Defend Military Tribunals for Terrorist Suspects," New York Times, November 15, 2001, at B6.

174. Id.

175. William P. Barr and Andrew G. McBride, "Military Justice for al Qaeda," Washington Post, November 18, 2001, at B7.

176. "Closer Look at New Plan for Trying Terrorists," New York Times, November 15, 2001, at B6.

177. "White House Push on Security Steps Bypasses Congress," New York Times, November 15, 2001, at A1.

Douglas Kmiec, another former OLC head, defended military tribunals by noting that neither the hearsay rule nor "ill-fitting" exclusionary rules would "derail the admission of evidence obtained under the interrogation authorized by the president." Curiously, he claimed that tribunals "are not primarily for punishment."[178] Most observers and practitioners regard tribunals as an expeditious way of determining guilt and meting out sentences, particularly the death penalty. Historically, tribunals have functioned as instruments for punishment, not exoneration.

Among those concerned that a military tribunal might jeopardize individual rights, many acquiesced because they feared the kind of televised trial that had resulted in the acquittal of O. J. Simpson. For example, Stewart A. Baker, a Washington attorney and former general counsel to the National Security Agency, remarked, "I don't think anyone wants to see Osama bin Laden brought before a court here to be defended by Johnnie Cochran."[179]

Opposition. Criticism of the Bush military order centered on its scope, the absence of procedural safeguards, and the concentration of power within the executive branch. Kevin Ernst, a Detroit lawyer representing an individual arrested for fraudulent immigration documents and jailed for twenty-five days before being released, said he had "no idea they were going to try to use it for domestically detained people. It scares the hell out of me, I'll tell you that."[180]

Senator Patrick Leahy (D-Vt.), chairman of the Judiciary Committee, said that he and other lawmakers had learned about the tribunal by reading the newspapers: "We're really not being consulted at all, and it's hard to understand why."[181] Leahy is considered a liberal Democrat, but the same comment was made by a conser-

178. "Douglas W. Kmiec, "Military Tribunals Are Necessary in Times of War," Wall Street Journal, November 15, 2001, at 26.
179. "Assurances Offered About Military Courts," New York Times, November 16, 2001, at B10.
180. "Senior Administration Officials Defend Military Tribunals for Terrorist Suspects," New York Times, November 15, 2001, at B6.
181. "White House Push on Security Steps Bypasses Congress," New York Times, November 15, 2001, at A1.

vative Republican, Representative Bob Barr of Georgia. As a member of the House Judiciary Committee, he remarked that he was not aware "that they're consulting us at all."[182] Leahy also worried that other nations would use military tribunals against American citizens, sending "a message to the world that it is acceptable to hold secret trials and summary executions without the possibility of judicial review, at least when the defendant is a foreign national."[183] An editorial in the *Washington Post* cautioned that when Americans are accused of terrorism in "secret courts by hooded judges in Peru or other nations, the U.S. Government rightly objects."[184]

A conservative Republican, William Safire of the *New York Times*, wrote a series of op-ed articles excoriating the military tribunal. He charged that Bush, "misadvised by a frustrated and panic-stricken attorney general," had seized dictatorial powers with his military order. A tribunal could operate by concealing evidence with arguments about national security, "make up its own rules, find a defendant guilty even if a third of the officers disagree, and execute the alien with no review by a civilian court."[185]

Senator Arlen Specter (R-Pa.) called for hearings to question why the White House was "bypassing Congress and unilaterally expanding its powers." Leahy agreed,[186] and on November 28, the Senate Judiciary Committee held hearings on "DOJ Oversight: Preserving Our Freedoms While Defending Against Terrorism." Leahy's opening statement said that the Administration, rather than "respect the checks and balances that make up our constitutional framework," chose to "cut out Congress in determining the appropriate tribunal and procedures to try terrorists." He warned that the military tribunal authorized by Bush could become "a template for

182. Id. at B7.
183. Id.
184. "End-Running the Bill of Rights," Washington Post, November 16, 2001, at A46.
185. William Safire, "Seizing Dictatorial Power," New York Times, November 15, 2001, at A31; see also his "Kangaroo Courts," New York Times, November 26, 2001, at A19.
186. "Assurances Offered about Military Courts," New York Times, November 16, 2001, at B10.

use by foreign governments against Americans overseas." Several expert witnesses appeared to testify both for and against the military tribunal.[187]

On December 4, the Senate Judiciary Committee held hearings to take testimony from other constitutional experts on such issues as whether Congress needed to pass legislation to authorize the tribunal and determine its procedures.[188] Two days later, the Committee met again, this time to hear from Attorney General Ashcroft. His prepared statement made it clear that those who voiced their opposition to the Administration gave aid and comfort to the terrorists:

We need honest, reasoned debate, and not fear-mongering. To those who pit Americans against immigrants and citizens against noncitizens, to those who scare peace-loving people with phantoms of lost liberty, my message is this: Your tactics only aid terrorists, for they erode our national unity and diminish our resolve. They give ammunition to America's enemies, and pause to America's friends.[189]

Who decides what is "honest" and "reasoned"? The Administration? How much does the quest for "national unity" discourage the individual voice? The executive branch can claim no monopoly on wisdom.

A day after the hearing, the Justice Department announced that Ashcroft did not intend to discourage public debate. What he found unhelpful to the country were "misstatements and the spread of misinformation about the actions of the Justice Department."[190] Yet the Administration itself—as with any Administration—has made its share of "misstatements." At the Senate Judiciary hearings, Ashcroft claimed that the President's authority to establish military

187. "Justice Dept. and Senate Clash over Bush Actions," New York Times, November 29, 2001, at B7l.

188. "Bush Defends Wartime Call for Tribunals," New York Times, December 5, 2001, at A1, B7.

189. "Excerpts from Attorney General's Testimony before Senate Judiciary Committee," New York Times, December 7, 2001, at B6. See also "Ashcroft Defends Antiterror Plan; Says Criticism May Aid U.S. Foes," New York Times, December 7, 2001, at A1.

190. "Ashcroft Aide Says Criticism Wasn't Aimed at Policy Foes," Washington Post, December 8, 2001, at A11.

tribunals "arises out of his power as Commander-in-Chief. For centuries, Congress has recognized this authority and the Supreme Court has never held that any Congress may limit it." Ashcroft appeared to claim that tribunals are created under the exclusive authority of the President and that, according to judicial precedents, Congress may not limit that authority. The legal and historical record of military tribunals presents quite a different picture: the creation of tribunals is typically done jointly by Congress and the President, Congress has not recognized a unilateral presidential authority to create these tribunals, and the Supreme Court has repeatedly held that Congress has the constitutional authority to create tribunals, decide their authorities and jurisdiction, and limit the President if he acts unilaterally by military order or proclamation to create these tribunals.[191] In the face of this record, does it make any sense to suggest that Ashcroft's "misstatements and the spread of misinformation" give aid to terrorists?

The war against terrorism does not justify any weakening of the constitutional rights of free speech and free press. It is particularly during war that free speech and public debate must be respected and encouraged. During World War I, Zechariah Chafee, Jr., convinced Justice Oliver Wendell Holmes, Jr., that the war clauses of the Constitution cannot break down the freedom of speech. It is in time of war that the government must be "vigorously and constantly cross-examined, so that the fundamental issues of the struggle may be clearly defined, and the war may not be diverted to improper ends, or conducted with an undue sacrifice of life and liberty, or prolonged after its just purposes are accomplished."[192]

Although Bush had authorized the military tribunal to try members

191. For example, 1 Ops. Att'y Gen. 233 (1818); 11 Ops. Att'y Gen. 297 (1865); William Winthrop, Military Law and Precedents 831 (New York: Arno Press, 2000); Ex parte Milligan, 71 U.S. 2, 121–22 (1866); Coleman v. Tennessee, 97 U.S. 509, 514 (1878); Ex parte Quirin, 317 U.S. 1, 28–29 (1942); In re Yamashita, 327 U.S. 1, 10–11, 16, 23 (1946); Duncan v. Kahanamoku, 327 U.S. 304 (1946); Madsen v. Kinsella, 343 U.S. 341, 348–49 (1952).

192. Zechariah Chafee, Jr., "Freedom of Speech in War Time," 32 Harvard Law Review 932, 958 (1919); Louis Fisher, American Constitutional Law (4th ed.) 486–87 (Durham, N.C.: Carolina Academic Press, 2001).

of al Qaeda, the Administration decided instead to indict Zacarias Moussaoui, a French citizen charged with being part of the Osama bin Laden conspiracy that crashed jetliners into the World Trade Center and the Pentagon. Observers thought that Moussaoui was precisely the type of person the Administration had had in mind when it created the military tribunal, yet it chose to prosecute through a federal grand jury and the regular civil courts.[193] Senator Joseph I. Lieberman (D-Conn.) asked, "If we will not try Zacarias Moussaoui before a military tribunal, who will we try in a military tribunal?"[194] The Administration believed that he might have been intended as the twentieth hijacker.

American Bar Association Study. A Task Force on Terrorism and the Law, organized by the American Bar Association (ABA), issued a January 4, 2002, report on military commissions. It concluded that the Bush military order raised many important issues of constitutional and international policy, creating a "potential reach quite broad" for which there is "no clear, controlling precedent."[195] Of particular concern to the task force was the order's broad sweep covering all noncitizens. Aliens in the United States consist of two groups: those present lawfully and those present unlawfully. The first group includes "lawful permanent residents; nonimmigrants (such as diplomats, and temporary visitors for work, study, or pleasure); and certain persons in humanitarian categories." The second category includes "undocumented aliens, that is, persons who entered the United States without authorization or inspection and who have not acquired lawful status; and status violators, that is, persons who entered the United States with authorization but who overstayed a visa or otherwise violated the terms of admission."[196]

193. "U.S. Indicts Suspect in Sept. 11 Attacks," Washington Post, December 12, 2001, at A1.
194. "Senators Ask: Why No Tribunal for Suspect?" Washington Post, December 13, 2001, at A14.
195. American Bar Association, Task Force on Terrorism and the Law, Report and Recommendations on Military Commissions, January 4, 2002, at 1.
196. Id. at 9 n.21.

Aliens: lawfully + unlawfully

The task force pointed out that aliens not within the United States have "few, if any, constitutional protections," while aliens present within the United States "are entitled to due process protections."[197] For that reason, subjecting non-U.S. citizens outside the United States to the jurisdiction of military tribunals "raises the least likelihood of constitutional impediments, and also appears less objectionable on policy grounds. With respect to aliens already in the United States, such jurisdiction raises much more serious questions."[198]

As to the section of the Bush order that appeared to deny defendants access to civil courts, the task force noted that the broad language "does not expressly suspend the writ of habeas corpus, and it is most unlikely that it could."[199] The task force pointed to such cases as *Quirin* and *Yamashita,* in which defendants had brought their applications for writs of habeas corpus to the Supreme Court. If the Bush order led to a trial before a military commission, "it can be assumed that the validity of the order and the jurisdiction of such commissions will be reviewed in federal courts—at least with respect to any persons or trials within the United States, if the defendant has legal counsel who seeks review notwithstanding the prohibitory language of the President's order."[200]

The task force recommended that military tribunals "should be limited to narrow circumstances in which compelling security interests justify their use." The task force concluded that, unless specifically authorized by Congress, the following persons should not be tried by military tribunals: "persons lawfully present in the United States; persons in the United States suspected or accused of offenses unconnected with the September 11 attacks; and persons not suspected or accused of violations of the law of war."[201] Further, the task force recommended that the procedures adopted for military tribunals should be guided by the appropriate principles of

197. Id. at 9–10.
198. Id. at 10.
199. Id. at 11.
200. Id.
201. Id. at 16.

law and rules of procedures and evidence prescribed for courts-martial, and should conform to Article 14 of the International Covenant on Civil and Political Rights. Included within Article 14 are provisions for an independent and impartial tribunal, open to the press and public (except for specific and compelling reasons), and various rights for the defendant, including presumption of innocence, prompt notice of charges, adequate time and facilities to prepare a defense, trial without undue delay, and other procedural safeguards. Moreover, anyone tried by a military tribunal in the United States "should be permitted to seek habeas corpus relief in United States courts."[202]

Defense Department Regulations. The Department of Defense (DOD) took the ABA study and other recommendations into account in preparing detailed procedures for military commissions. Those procedures were released on March 21, 2002, as Military Commission Order No. 1. At a news briefing that day, DOD General Counsel William J. Haynes II cited the 1942 decision in *Quirin* for legal support. The Supreme Court, he said, had "found that the president's order in that case was constitutional and properly applied."

The March 21 order changed some of the procedures included in the Bush order of November 13, 2001. The responsibility for appointing military commissions falls to the Secretary of Defense "or a designee." The commissions established under this authority "shall have jurisdiction over violations of the laws of war and all other offenses triable by military commission." A commission shall consist of at least three but no more than seven members, each of them a commissioned officer of the U.S. armed forces. The Presiding Officer of the commission, who must be a judge advocate of any U.S. armed force, is responsible for admitting or excluding evidence.

The Chief Prosecutor shall be a judge advocate of any U.S. armed force. The Defense Counsel shall also be a judge advocate

202. Id. at 17.

of any U.S. armed force, but the accused may retain the services of
a civilian attorney, at no expense to the U.S. government, provided
that the attorney is a U.S. citizen and meets certain other criteria
detailed in the order. The accused shall be "presumed innocent
until proven guilty." In finding a vote of guilty, a commission member must be convinced "beyond a reasonable doubt." The accused
is not required to testify during the trial, and the commission may
not draw "adverse inference" from the accused's decision not to
testify. If the accused elects to testify, the accused shall be subject
to cross-examination.

The accused may obtain witnesses and documents for the accused's defense, "to the extent necessary and reasonably available"
as determined by the Presiding Officer. The accused may be present
at every stage of the trial, unless the accused engages in disruptive
conduct that justifies exclusion by the Presiding Officer. The Defense Counsel may not be excluded from any portion of the trial
proceeding. The accused is entitled to a trial open to the public, although the Presiding Officer has the authority to close proceedings,
or portions of proceedings, in accordance with the procedures set
forth in the order.

Instead of the two-thirds majority required to convict and sentence in the Bush military order, the two-thirds vote is retained for
conviction, but a sentence of death requires "a unanimous, affirmative vote of all of the members." Although three to seven officers sit
on tribunals, for death penalty cases, seven officers are required.
Whereas under the Bush order the trial record would go directly
from the tribunal to the President or to the Secretary of Defense, the
March 21 regulations require a three-member review panel appointed by the Secretary of Defense. At least one member shall
have experience as a judge, and civilians may also be commissioned to serve on the review panel. Within thirty days, the review
panel shall either forward the case to the Secretary of Defense with
a recommendation as to its disposition or return the case to the appointing authority for further proceedings, provided that a majority
of the review panel "has formed a definite and firm conviction that a
material error of law occurred."

The Secretary of Defense shall review the trial record and the recommendation of the review panel, either returning the case for further proceedings or forwarding it to the President with a recommendation as to its disposition. The case then goes to the President for review and final decision unless the President designates the Secretary to perform that function. At the news briefing on March 21, DOD General Counsel Haynes acknowledged that "somebody could be tried and acquitted of that charge, but may not necessarily automatically be released." When questioned about the exclusion of the Supreme Court from the review process, Undersecretary of Defense Douglas Feith responded, "I don't think you'll find anything that excludes the Supreme—it's not within our power to exclude the Supreme Court from the process. . . . As far as whether the Supreme Court gets involved in the process, that's beyond our authority to say." Haynes added, "Far be it from me to tell the Supreme Court not to do something."

Conclusions

The legal mind has a lazy habit of looking for "precedents" to justify what has been done or is about to be done. Little effort is made to scrutinize the precedent to determine whether it was acceptable then or worth repeating. The fact that something has been done before does not mean it should be done again. There is nothing "apt" about the *Quirin* decision.[1] As Justice Frankfurter later remarked, it "was not a happy precedent."[2] The American legal system would do well not to see its like again.

Did the eight Germans arriving in the United States in time of war, prepared to commit sabotage for an enemy power, have a constitutional right to a jury trial in civil court? No. Does it therefore follow that President Roosevelt's proclamation and military order satisfied statutory and constitutional standards? Not necessarily. A jury trial in civil court remains an option, as the Bush Administration demonstrated by trying Zacarias Moussaoui in civil court. Many factors, practical and legal, may dictate litigation through the regular courts. Citing *Quirin* as a precedent does not justify its repetition. There were many flaws in the procedures used by the military tribunal and in the decision-making process of the Court. Alternatives more in keeping with American legal values were available in 1942 and remain so today.

1. William P. Barr and Andrew G. McBride, "Military Justice for al Qaeda," Washington Post, November 18, 2001, at B7.

2. Memorandum Re: *Rosenberg* v. *United States,* Nos. 111 and 687, October Term 1952," June 4, 1953, at 8, Frankfurter Papers, Harvard Law School, Part I, Reel 70, LC.

The Nazi saboteur case represented an unwise and ill-conceived concentration of power in the executive branch. Roosevelt appointed the tribunal and served as the final reviewing authority. "Crimes" related to the law of war came not from the legislative branch, enacted by statute, but from executive interpretations of the "law of war." Throughout the six weeks of the trial by military tribunal and the habeas corpus petition to the Supreme Court, Congress was not a participant. The judiciary was largely shut out as well. The two days of oral argument before the Court were dramatic and newsworthy but hardly a check on presidential power.

Important constitutional principles were placed before the Court, but the main focus was not the rights of the accused. Roosevelt had thrown down the gauntlet at the Justices by denying the saboteurs access to civil remedies. The Court wanted to make a statement that it has a reviewing function in time of war as well as peace. To be circumvented or stiff-armed by the President did damage to the prestige, dignity, and reputation of the judiciary. There was little expectation that the Court would do anything other than what it did: deny the petition for a writ of habeas corpus. Roosevelt and Biddle could tolerate that level of judicial participation, but no more. There was no reason to think that the Court would go further and actually examine the facts of the case, look critically at procedural irregularities, pass judgment on guilt or innocence, or rebuff the President.

The purpose of trying the eight Germans in secret was not to protect military secrets or safeguard national security. The need for secrecy was driven by two reasons: to conceal the fact that Dasch had turned himself (and the others) in, and to mete out the death penalty. Most of the trial could have been conducted openly, with the public and the press invited, without sacrificing any legitimate national interests. On the rare occasions when sensitive data might have been revealed, the courtroom could have been cleared for that part of the testimony.

Roosevelt's creation of the military commission was deeply flawed. It was a mistake to have the Judge Advocate General share prosecutorial duties with the Attorney General. The Judge Advocate General adds integrity to the system of military justice by serving as a reviewing authority, not as a prosecutor. Whatever the military tribunal decided should have come for review to the Judge Advocate General and his staff, acting in an independent capacity, and then to the President for possible clemency. The trial record should never have gone directly to the President, as Roosevelt provided in his order of July 2, 1942. Neither Roosevelt nor any other President is in a position to read a 3,000-page trial transcript with the requisite care and legal judgment.

It was error for Roosevelt to authorize the tribunal to "make such rules for the conduct of the proceeding, consistent with the powers of military commissions under the Articles of War, as it shall deem necessary for a full and fair trial of the matters before it." Procedural rules need to be agreed to before a trial begins, not after. No confidence can be placed in rules created on the spot, particularly when done in secret. It would have been better for the military tribunal to operate under the procedures set forth in the Articles of War and the *Manual for Courts-Martial.* Those procedures were in place and represented the product of mature thought and careful study over a long period of time. With their statutory base, they would have given congressional sanction to the process and removed the impression of executive arbitrariness.

The language in Roosevelt's proclamation, prohibiting access to civil courts, created a needless confrontation with the Supreme Court and forced it to assert itself and protect judicial prerogatives. Had Roosevelt created a tribunal and directed it to follow the statutory procedures available in the Articles of War, including internal review of the record by the Judge Advocate General, the civil courts would have been in a position to more comfortably deny jurisdiction to any petition for a writ of habeas corpus. Drafting the proclamation as he did, Roosevelt practically compelled the Court to take the case and pretend to exercise an independent review, when all knowledgeable observers knew what the outcome would be.

Assembling the Court in the middle of the summer in emergency session, with briefs hurriedly prepared and read, sent a message of inconsiderateness, not careful judicial deliberation. Nine hours of oral argument highlighted the lack of preparation. Taking the case

directly from the district court, without intervening review by the
D.C. Circuit, further underscored the rush to judgment. The petition
for certiorari reached the Court a few minutes before it convened,
granted certiorari, and announced its per curiam decision. This
hastily drafted per curiam was followed by the execution of six of
the Germans. Not until almost three months later did the Court
manage to issue its full opinion, offering belated reasons and constitutional analysis.

The reasons and analysis, strained and uninformed in many
places, were compromised by the political situation the Court found
itself in. It had to make a decision without knowing how the secret
trial was being conducted or how it would turn out. The Justices
knew that information unavailable to them would be released
within a few years, putting the Court's reputation at risk. Nothing in
the decision could imply, in any way, that there had been a miscarriage of justice. The customary airing of individual views through
concurrences and dissents could not be allowed. The multiple problems of _Quirin_ and the military trial would later be exposed by
Frederick Bernays Wiener and other scholars.

Secretary of War Stimson had objected to the participation of Attorney General Biddle and Judge Advocate General Cramer as prosecutors in 1942. Stimson also disliked the drama of a trial held in
the Justice Department. When the need for a military tribunal resur-
faced in 1945, he was this time successful in preventing Biddle and
Cramer from serving as prosecutors. Stimson prevailed in having
the trial located at Governors Island, instead of the nation's capital,
and in keeping Cramer in his statutory role as a reviewing officer
within JAG. Stimson raised other objections to the 1942 procedure,
such as having the trial record go directly to the President. In 1945,
he corrected that deficiency by having the trial record go first to
General Terry and from there to JAG. Instead of having the President appoint tribunal members and counsel, as in 1942, those duties
were vested in General Terry.

One of the strange stories after the war was a 1945 interview
with Maj. Gen. Erwin Lahousen, who had directed German sabotage operations. He said that when Hitler, who had personally ordered

operation Pastorian

CONCLUSIONS 175

"Operation Pastorius," learned how quickly the eight men had been picked up, he yelled at Germany's intelligence chiefs: "Why didn't you take Jews for that?"[3] The story can be interpreted in several ways, such as that Jews were regarded as expendable for such operations. But as a result of Hitler's outburst, Jews received jobs in the German Intelligence Service for more than a year. Thus, the more likely interpretation is that regardless of Hitler's morbid anti-Semitism, he respected Jews for their intelligence and competence.

In 1948, President Truman commuted the sentences of Dasch and Burger and sent them back to Germany. Attorney General Tom Clark recommended clemency for the two, suggesting that it was a good idea to let foreign agents engaged in espionage or sabotage know that they have "everything to gain" by unmasking plots against the United States.[4] An Army transport landed both men in Bremerhaven, Germany, to live in the American zone under suspended sentences and under restrictions to be devised by the American Military Governor.[5]

Without September 11 and the Bush military order of November 13, 2001, *Quirin* might be remembered as a curious artifact of World War II. Experts in military law would recall it, but not too well. It is now front and center, to be understood within the context of American constitutional law, the relations between Congress and the President, and the tradition of an independent judiciary. We are all familiar with the extent to which legal principles are sacrificed in time of war. How much can we learn from the 1942–1945 experience to avoid duplicating mistakes?

3. "German Bares Aid in '42 U-boat Plot," New York Times, October 10, 1945, at 1.

4. "2 Nazi Saboteurs Freed by Truman," New York Times, April 27, 1948, at 9.

5. Id.; memorandum from President Harry Truman to the Attorney General and the Secretary of the Army, March 20, 1948, RG 60, General Records of the Department of Justice, Box 19, National Archives, College Park, Md.

overtay h authory

Chronology

April 1942	Training of saboteurs at a farm near Brandenburg, Germany.
May	Twelve-day vacation, followed by a tour of canal locks, railroad yards, and aluminum plants in Berlin; train to Paris and to submarine base at Lorient, France.
May 26	Kerling's group leaves by submarine.
May 28	Dasch's group leaves by submarine.
June 13	Dasch's team lands at Amagansett, Long Island, N.Y.
June 17	Kerling's team lands at Ponte Vedra, near Jacksonville, Fla.
June 19	Dasch taken into protective custody by the FBI, Washington, D.C.
June 20	Quirin, Heinck, and Burger arrested by the FBI, New York City.
June 23	Kerling and Thiel arrested by the FBI, New York City.
June 27	Haupt and Neubauer arrested by the FBI, Chicago, Ill.
July 2	President Roosevelt issues proclamation creating military tribunal.
July 8	Military trial begins in Room 5235 of the Department of Justice.
July 21	Defense counsel Royall informs tribunal that he intends to apply for a writ of habeas corpus in U.S. district court to test the constitutionality of the President's proclamation.

July 23	Royall, Dowell, Biddle, and Cramer fly to Justice Roberts's farm, outside Philadelphia; Chief Justice Stone agrees to hear the case.
July 27	Supreme Court publicly announces it will hear the case.
July 28	District court rejects Royall's petition for a writ of habeas corpus.
July 29–30	Oral argument before the U.S. Supreme Court.
July 31	Military trial resumes at 10:00. At noon, the Supreme Court upholds the jurisdiction of the military tribunal to try the defendants.
August 1	Military trial concludes.
August 3	Military tribunal reaches verdict; court papers are submitted to Roosevelt.
August 4	Custodian Cox informed that six of the Germans will be electrocuted.
August 8	Roosevelt publicly approves tribunal's judgment that all eight are guilty; six are electrocuted; Dasch and Burger receive prison sentences.
November 29, 1944	Colepaugh and Gimpel come ashore on the coast of Maine.
December 30, 1944	They are apprehended.
February 14, 1945	Military tribunal sentences Colepaugh and Gimpel to die by hanging.
June 23, 1945	President Truman commutes their sentences to life imprisonment.
April 26, 1948	President Truman commutes the sentences of Dasch and Burger and sends them to Germany.
August 12, 1955	Gimpel, released from prison, is deported to Germany.
1960	Colepaugh is released from prison.

Major Participants

Adm. Wilhelm Canaris, head of Abwehr

Col. Erwin von Lahousen, chief of Sabotage Division, Abwehr

Lt. Walter Kappe, director of sabotage school

Eight saboteurs: George John Dasch, Ernest Peter Burger, Heinrich Harm Heinck, Richard Quirin, Edward John Kerling, Hermann Neubauer, Werner Thiel, Herbert Haupt

Secretary of War Henry L. Stimson

Members of the military commisson: Maj. Gen. Frank R. McCoy, President, Maj. Gen. Walter S. Grant, Maj. Gen. Blanton Winship, Maj. Gen. Lorenzo D. Gasser, Brig. Gen. Guy V. Henry, Brig. Gen. John T. Lewis, Brig. Gen. John T. Kennedy

Prosecutors and members of the government: Attorney General Francis Biddle; Maj. Gen. Myron Cramer, Judge Advocate General (JAG), U.S. Army; Col. F. Granville Munson, JAG officer; Col. John M. Weir, JAG officer; Col. Erwin M. Treusch, JAG officer; Oscar Cox, Assistant Solicitor General; James H. Rowe, Jr., Assistant to the Solicitor General; Brig. Gen. Albert L. Cox, Provost Marshal

Counsel for the accused (except Dasch): Col. Cassius M. Dowell, Col. Kenneth Royall, Maj. Lauson H. Stone, Capt. William G. Hummell

Counsel for Dasch: Col. Carl L. Ristine

William C. Colepaugh

Erich Gimpel

Bibliographical Essay

The main treasure trove for conducting research on the Nazi saboteurs is the trial transcript of the military tribunal, which heard evidence and argument from July 8 to August 1, 1942. The transcript consists of 2,967 pages (legal size) in three boxes at the National Archives, College Park, Maryland, under "RG 153, Records of the Office of the Judge Advocate General (Army), Court-Martial Case Files, CM 334178, 1942 German Saboteur Case." It took me ten full (but exhilarating) days to read this material, take notes, and make photocopies of selected pages, sticking to the task from 8:45 a.m. to 9 p.m. on most days, or until the closing time of 5 p.m. on other days. The trial transcript is stored in Boxes 17, 18, and 19, with some correspondence kept at the end of Box 19. Boxes 20 and 21 contain other correspondence on such matters as applications for pardons and clemency for George John Dasch and Ernest Peter Burger. Copies of the trial transcript are available elsewhere, such as the FDR Library.

Also valuable are the petitions, briefs, and oral argument before the Supreme Court in Ex parte Quirin, all of which are published in Volume 39 of Landmark Briefs and Arguments of the Supreme Court of the United States: Constitutional Law, edited by Philip B. Kurland and Gerhard Casper (Arlington, Va.: University Publications of America, 1975). The nine hours of oral argument run from pages 496 to 666. The Court's July 31 per curiam in Ex parte Quirin appears at 63 S.Ct. 1 (1942), its full opinion at 317 U.S. 1 (1942), and the district court ruling at 47 F.Supp. 43 (D.D.C. 1942).

Roosevelt's proclamation and military order creating the military commission for the eight Germans and appointing the members of the commission and the defense counsel appear in the *Federal Register*, vol. 7, pp. 5101, 5103 (1942). I also read floor statements by members of Congress that appeared in the *Congressional Record* for 1942. Significant opinions by the Attorney General on presidential authority to create military courts and military commissions are published in *Official Opinions of the Attorneys General of the United States,* vol. 1, pp. 233–44 (September 14, 1818); vol. 11, pp. 297–317 (July 1865); vol. 14, pp. 249–53 (June 7, 1873); vol. 16, pp. 292–95 (March 26, 1879); vol. 31, pp. 356–65 (November 25, 1918); and vol. 40, pp. 561–62 (December 24, 1919).

I read the papers of the Justices who decided *Ex parte Quirin,* relying on the manuscript collections at the Library of Congress for Harlan Fiske Stone, who served as Chief Justice at that time, as well as Hugo Black, William O. Douglas, Felix Frankfurter, and Robert H. Jackson. Those documents chronicle the slow and painful development of Stone's opinion for the Court. I appreciate the assistance of Hugo Black, Jr., for giving me access to his father's papers. My appreciation also to the library of Clemson University for the papers of Justice James F. Byrnes, the library of the University of Kentucky for the papers of Justice Stanley Reed, and the Seeley G. Mudd Library, Princeton University, for a conversation between Justice Douglas and Professor Walter F. Murphy. Justice Frank Murphy did not participate in the case. Justice Owen Roberts, who played a key role in arranging for oral argument, destroyed his files of particular cases. Also in the manuscript room of the Library of Congress, I read the insightful diary of Secretary of War Henry L. Stimson and the papers of Frank Ross McCoy, who served as president of the military tribunal in 1942. At the FDR Library, I read documents from the papers of Francis Biddle, Oscar Cox, and other participants in the military tribunal.

Many of the saboteurs were active in such American organizations as Friends for New Germany and the German-American Bund. For background on these groups, one can read *Outline of Evidence: German-American Bund (Amerikadeutscher Volksbund),* prepared by the Criminal Division of the U.S. Department of Justice, September 17, 1942; Sander A. Diamond, *The Nazi Movement in the United States, 1924–1941* (Ithaca, N.Y.: Cornell University Press, 1974); and Susan Canedy, *America's Nazis: A Democratic Dilemma* (Menlo Park, Calif.: Markgraf, 1990).

To gauge public reaction to the saboteur arrests and trial, I read the *New York Times* and the *Washington Post* from June 28 through August 13, 1942. I continued to read articles in the *New York Times* up to 1957 to follow the arrests, sentencing, and commutation of sentences of family and friends of the eight Germans. I also read articles in the *Chicago Daily Tribune* and the *Los Angeles Times.* In addition to newspaper coverage, I read articles during that period in such magazines as *Life, New Republic, Newsweek, Saturday Review of Literature,* and *Time.*

For excellent background on German espionage in America, see Ladislas

Farago, *The Game of the Foxes: The Untold Story of German Espionage in the United States and Great Britain During World War II* (New York: David McKay, 1971), and David Kahn, *Hitler's Spies: German Military Intelligence in World War II* (New York: Macmillan, 1978). Covering the same topic but with greater focus on the 1942 saboteur effort is Alan Hynd, *Passport to Treason: The Inside Story of Spies in America* (New York: Robert M. McBride, 1943). Loaded with errors, it praises the detective work of the FBI on almost every page without once mentioning that Dasch gave himself up. Another account of the 1942 saboteur effort is by Chargles Wighton and Günter Peis, *They Spied on England: Based on the German Secret Service War Diary of General von Lahousen* (London: Odhams Press, 1958). It contains valuable excerpts from Lahousen's diary but is marred by wrong names, ages, dates, hotels, and restaurants and an imaginary meeting between Dasch and FBI Director Hoover.

Eugene Rachlis wrote a fine book, *They Came to Kill: The Story of Eight Saboteurs in America* (New York: Random House, 1961). The title is somewhat of a misnomer, because the eight Germans were directed not to kill Americans. Rachlis had access to the trial records and enriched his book with newpaper stories, interviews, and personal correspondence. The other book-length treatment is by George J. Dasch, *Eight Spies Against America* (New York: Robert M. McBride, 1959), which represents his version of why he was denied justice. The introduction states that Dasch "was one of the great heroes of World War II." Unsuccessfully, he tries to substantiate that image.

The work of the military tribunal and the Supreme Court's decision in *Ex parte Quirin* received extensive coverage at the time in law reviews and political science journals. Some of the pieces were written by participants, such as by Gen. Myron C. Cramer, Judge Advocate General, U.S. Army, who prosecuted the case with Attorney General Biddle. Cramer's article is entitled "Military Commissions: Trial of the Eight Saboteurs," 17 *Washington Law Review and State Bar Journal* 247 (November 1942). Another participant was Col. F. Granville Munson from the Judge Advocate General's Department. His article: "The Arguments in the Saboteur Trial," 91 *University of Pennsylvania Law Review* 239 (November 1942).

Other scholarly treatments include: Robert E. Cushman, "*Ex parte Quirin et al.*—The Nazi Saboteur Case," 28 *Cornell Law Quarterly* 54 (November 1942); Notes: "Jurisdiction of Military Tribunals," 37 *Illinois Law Review* 265 (November–December 1942); George T. Schilling, "Saboteurs and the Jurisdiction of Military Commissions," 41 *Michigan Law Review* 481 (December 1942); Robert E. Cushman, "The Case of the Nazi Saboteurs," 36 *American Political Science Review* 1082 (December 1942); Charles Cheney Hyde,

"Aspects of the Saboteur Cases," 37 *American Journal of International Law* 88 (January 1943); Note, "Federal Military Commissions: Procedure and 'Wartime Base' of Jurisdiction," 56 *Harvard Law Review* 631 (January 1943); and Cyrus Bernstein, "The Saboteur Trial: A Case History," 11 *George Washington Law Review* 131 (February 1943).

Albert L. Cox, the jailer and custodian of the eight Germans, wrote "The Saboteur Story," *Records of the Columbia History Society of Washington, D.C.,* 1957–1959, pp. 16–25. Francis Biddle, who argued the case as Attorney General, devotes Chapter 21 to the German saboteurs in his book *In Brief Authority* (Garden City, N.Y.: Doubleday, 1962). Leon O. Prior, an FBI agent who testified at the saboteur trial and served as a guard for Ernest Peter Burger, wrote "Nazi Invasion of Florida," 49 *Florida Historical Quarterly* 129 (October 1970). Another short article is by W. A. Swanberg, "The Spies Who Came in from the Sea," 21 *American Heritage* 66 (April 1970).

William O. Douglas, one of the Justices who decided the case, discusses it in his book *The Court Years, 1939–1975* (New York: Vintage Books, 1981), pp. 138–39. Boris I. Bittker, who assisted the prosecution (and sometimes even the defense), wrote an engaging article in 1997 on the Court's jurisdictional dilemma of taking *Ex parte Quirin* directly from the district court without first receiving judgment by the appellate court, the D.C. Circuit: "The World War II German Saboteur's Case and Writs of Certiorari Before Judgment by the Court of Appeals: A Tale of Nunc Pro Tunc Jurisdiction," 14 *Constitutional Commentary* 431 (1997).

Other treatments of *Quirin* include: Samuel J. Konefsky, *Chief Justice Stone and the Supreme Court* (New York: Macmillan, 1945), pp. 236–45, and Edward S. Corwin, *Total War and the Constitution* (New York: Alfred A. Knopf, 1947), pp. 117–21. Samuel I. Rosenman, *Working with Roosevelt* (New York: Harper & Row, 1952), pp. 351–54, describes Roosevelt's mood on the evening after six of the Germans had been electrocuted. William D. Hassett, *Off the Record with F.D.R., 1942–1945* (New Brunswick, N.J.: Rutgers University Press, 1958), pp. 74–75, 83, 86, 90, 97–99, discusses Roosevelt's reactions to the arrests of the saboteurs, the trial, and whether they should be shot or hanged.

A major analysis of Chief Justice Stone's effort to craft *Quirin* is by Alpheus Thomas Mason, first appearing in "Inter Arma Silent Leges: Chief Justice Stone's Views," 69 *Harvard Law Review* 806 (1956), and later as a chapter in his book *Harlan Fiske Stone: Pillar of the Law* (New York: Viking Press, 1956), pp. 653–719. Bennett Boskey, who served as law clerk to Stone, thought that Mason may have published his views too early, since four Justices of the *Quirin* Court were still on the bench in 1956. Boskey's article: "A Justice's Papers; Chief Justice Stone's Biographer and the Saboteurs' Case," 14 *Supreme Court Historical Society Quarterly* 10 (1993).

Other articles are highly perceptive in analyzing the law and politics of the case: Michal R. Belknap, "The Supreme Court Goes to War: The Meaning and Implications of the Nazi Saboteur Case," 89 *Military Law Review* 59 (1980); Michal Belknap, "Frankfurter and the Nazi Saboteurs," *Yearbook 1982: Supreme Court Historical Society,* 66–71; David J. Danelski, "The Saboteurs' Case," 1 *Journal of Supreme Court History,* 61–82 (1996).

The Bush military order of November 13, 2001, stimulated a number of articles on *Quirin,* including Tony Mauro, "A Mixed Precedent for Military Tribunals," *Legal Times,* November 19, 2001, at 15; David G. Savage, "Military Trials Have Roots in Nazi Case," *Los Angeles Times,* November 19, 2001, at A2; Louis Fisher, "Bush Can't Rely on the FDR Precedent," *Los Angeles Times,* December 2, 2001, at M3; George Lardner, Jr., "Nazi Saboteurs Captured!" *Washington Post Magazine,* January 13, 2002, at 12–16, 23–24; Andy Newman, "Terrorists Among Us (Back in '42)," *New York Times,* January 17, 2002, at A26; Gary Cohen, "The Keystone Kommandos," *Atlantic Monthly,* February 2002, at 46–59; Hugh Latimer, "Tribunals and the Court: Misconstruing 'Quirin,'" *National Law Journal,* March 18, 2002, at A20; and Michal R. Belknap, "A Putrid Pedigree: The Bush Administration's Military Tribunals in Historical Perspective," 38 *California Western Law Review,* 433, 471–79 (2002).

Index of Cases

Subject Index